History of the Dominican Republic

A Captivating Guide to the Caribbean Island's Ancient Roots, Taínos and Caribs, Colonial Past, and Modern Times

CAPTIVATING HISTORY

Free Bonus from Captivating History (Available for a Limited time)

Hi History Lovers!

Now you have a chance to join our exclusive history list so you can get your first history ebook for free as well as discounts and a potential to get more history books for free!

Simply visit the link below to join.

Or, Scan the QR code!

captivatinghistory.com/ebook

Also, make sure to follow us on Facebook, X, and YouTube by searching for Captivating History.

Table of Contents

INTRODUCTION 1

CHAPTER 1 - BEFORE COLUMBUS - ANCIENT ROOTS 3

CHAPTER 2 - THE TAÍNOS AND CARIBS (KALINAGO) -
INDIGENOUS CIVILIZATIONS 10

CHAPTER 3 - ENCOUNTER AND CONQUEST...19

CHAPTER 4 - COLONIAL ERA AND THE SUGAR BOOM..........................26

CHAPTER 5 - PIRATES, SMUGGLERS, AND COLONIAL RIVALS..............36

CHAPTER 6 - STRUGGLE FOR SOVEREIGNTY...50

CHAPTER 7 - POLITICAL INSECURITY AND THE QUEST FOR
STABILITY...61

CHAPTER 8 - THE AMERICAN INTERVENTION AND TRUJILLO'S
DICTATORSHIP 72

CHAPTER 9 - THE PATH TOWARD MODERN DEMOCRACY...................82

CHAPTER 10 - THE DOMINICAN REPUBLIC AND THE MODERN
ERA...89

CONCLUSION 93

HERE'S ANOTHER BOOK BY CAPTIVATING HISTORY THAT
YOU MIGHT LIKE...97

FREE BONUS FROM CAPTIVATING HISTORY (AVAILABLE FOR
A LIMITED TIME) 98

REFERENCES...99

Introduction

Nestled in the heart of the Caribbean, the Dominican Republic shares the island of Hispaniola with Haiti. The Dominican Republic easily claims a rich and tumultuous history shaped by indigenous cultures, European conquests, and the relentless tides of change and resilience. This isn't simply a tale of a single nation but a narrative deeply intertwined with the broader history of the Americas and the Caribbean. The Dominican Republic's unique journey reveals much about the complexities of colonialism, the struggles for independence, and the ongoing quest for national identity and stability.

The significance of the Dominican Republic in the broader Caribbean history is multifaceted. Geographically, it occupies a strategic position in the Antilles archipelago, commanding the historical Columbus passage between the North and South American continents. This pivotal location made Hispaniola a centerpiece in the colonial ambitions of Europe's great powers. The island was the first permanent European settlement in the Americas, the springboard from which the Spanish Empire expanded its territories in the New World. It became the location where European, African, and Indigenous American cultures met, clashed, and eventually blended. This eventually gave rise to a unique cultural and racial mosaic that continues to define the Dominican identity.

The Dominican Republic's history is characterized by a series of paradoxes. It's a land marked by the firsts of European colonialism, yet it also became one of the first to challenge and throw off colonial rule. It was the site of the earliest importation of African slaves in the Americas, yet it also became a melting pot where African, Indigenous, and European influences fused into a distinctive culture. This clash of cultures and identities is reflected in the country's music, art, literature, and societal norms. You can easily see the distinctly Dominican aspects and parts of a broader Caribbean and Latin American heritage.

Our aim is to unravel these complex layers, offering a comprehensive look into the Dominican Republic's history. We'll start from its earliest inhabitants and travel to its contemporary era, beginning with the ancient Taíno and Carib societies that flourished before the arrival of Europeans. We'll explore their way of life, beliefs, and the devastating impact of conquest and colonization. The colonial period, marked by Spanish rule, and the introduction of African slavery set the stage for the turbulent centuries that followed. Following this, we'll move on to the struggles for independence and sovereignty, the era of dictators like Rafael Trujillo, and the challenging path toward modern democracy.

Throughout its history, the Dominican Republic has navigated the challenges of defining itself amidst external influences and internal conflicts. The struggle against colonial powers, the turbulent relationship with Haiti, and the internal strife and dictatorships of the twentieth century have all contributed to a national identity that is resilient, proud, and continually evolving. The Dominican people's cultural expressions, from merengue and bachata to literature and visual arts, are imbued with these experiences, offering a rich tapestry of resilience and creativity that spreads far beyond the island's shores.

The Dominican Republic's history is a vivid illustration of the struggles and triumphs of a nation carving out its place in the world. It is a story of cultural fusion and the forging of a unique national identity. This book aims to bring that story to life. We want to offer readers an insightful journey through the past and present of this remarkable Caribbean nation. As we turn the pages, we start a journey not just through the history of a country but through the history of a people who have faced adversity with courage. We explore the lives and ancestry of people who made indelible contributions to our shared world history.

Chapter 1 – Before Columbus – Ancient Roots

To begin, we must explore the Dominican Republic's distant past, in the era before the arrival of Christopher Columbus and European influences. Our focus here is on the ancient roots of Hispaniola—the island now shared by the Dominican Republic and Haiti.

The geological story sets the stage for the environmental backdrop against which early human activities unfolded. By taking a quick look at the physical landscape, we gain insights into the challenges and opportunities faced by the island's first inhabitants. It also allows us to trace the migrations that led to its initial settlement. These early inhabitants, whose history is pieced together through archaeological findings and anthropological studies, laid the first human footprints on Hispaniola's diverse landscapes.

This period is often overshadowed by the dramatic events of the colonial age and is essential for a comprehensive grasp of the island's history. As we move through this chapter, we lay the groundwork for the successive waves of change that soon swept across Hispaniola with the arrival of Europeans.

The Geological Formation of Hispaniola

Hispaniola has a geological story as complex and fascinating as its human history. The formation of this island (which happens to be the second largest in the Caribbean) is a tale of tectonic movements, volcanic activity, and the relentless forces of nature that have shaped the landscape over millions of years.

The story of Hispaniola begins with the ancient supercontinent Pangaea, which encompassed most of the Earth's landmasses. Around 200 million years ago, this land mass began to fragment. Through this process, the Atlantic Ocean and the smaller landmasses surrounding it were formed. The Caribbean Plate was part of this dramatic geological rearrangement. The Caribbean Plate slid eastward and collided with the North American Plate. The movement of these plates led to the considerable volcanic activity that created the islands of the Caribbean that we know today.

The Cordillera Central is Hispaniola's most prominent mountain range and stretches across the heart of the Dominican Republic. You'll find that the elevations in this range are some of the highest in the area. This range was formed primarily during the Miocene epoch, around twenty million years ago.

What made the island appealing to traveling peoples was its fertile valleys and plains, a result of both volcanic deposits and sedimentation from rivers and streams. These rich alluvial deposits have been a boon for agriculture, a fact that drew the island's earliest human settlers to its shores.

Hispaniola's geological history has also been marked by significant seismic activity. The island sits at the intersection of the Caribbean and North American tectonic plates. The regular earthquakes caused by these plates not only shaped the island's topography but also influenced human settlements and historical developments.

The diverse topography of Hispaniola has created a range of microclimates and ecosystems. This environmental diversity has been a key factor in the development of the island's flora and fauna.

Environmental and Ecological Aspects of Early Hispaniola

Hispaniola's environmental and ecological landscape played a pivotal role in shaping the lives and cultures of its pre-Columbian inhabitants. The island, characterized by its varied topography, rich biodiversity, and distinct microclimates, offered a wealth of resources that the early societies skillfully utilized and managed.

Diverse Landscapes and Their Resources

Hispaniola's topography is marked by rugged mountains, rolling hills, fertile valleys, and coastal plains. Each of these landscapes offered different resources and posed unique challenges to the early inhabitants. The mountainous regions, primarily the Cordillera Central, were rich in mineral resources and hardwood forests. These forests provided timber for construction and fuel, as well as a habitat for various game species. The valleys, particularly the Cibao Valley, were fertile grounds ideal for agriculture. The rich soils of these valleys were well-suited for cultivating crops like cassava, maize, and a variety of fruits and vegetables.

The abundance of fish and other marine resources provided a reliable food source. The rivers not only offered fresh water for consumption and agriculture but also served as avenues for transportation and communication.

Climate and Weather Patterns

The climate of Hispaniola, tropical with regional variations, influenced agricultural cycles and resource availability. The island experiences a wet and a dry season, with variations in rainfall patterns across different regions. These climatic conditions affected the growing seasons, determining when and what crops could be cultivated. The early inhabitants had to understand and adapt to these climatic rhythms to ensure food security and sustainability.

Biodiversity and Its Utilization

The island's flora and fauna were diverse. A tight space full of a wide variety of ecosystems fostered a matching variety of flora and fauna for early settlers to take advantage of. The indigenous peoples utilized this biodiversity for food and for medicinal purposes. They had extensive knowledge of the medicinal properties of various plants and herbs, which they used to treat a range of ailments. This knowledge was integral to their survival and well-being.

Pre-Columbian Human Activity and Migrations

The story of pre-Columbian Hispaniola is not just a tale of the people who lived there. It's also about the migrations that brought them to this island. These migrations brought peoples to all the islands of the Caribbean through waves of voyages and eventually settlement as early as 400 BC.

The initial peopling of Hispaniola is directly related to the rest of the Americas. The prevailing theory suggests that the first inhabitants of the Americas arrived via the Bering land bridge from Asia. Over time, these people settled and had families. It's the descendants of these early peoples who made their way to the Caribbean islands. The earliest inhabitants of Hispaniola arrived by navigating through the island chain from the South American mainland. Considering the resources at hand, this is a remarkable feat of ancient seafaring.

These early migrants arrived in a world untouched by modern human activity, rich in resources, and ripe for settlement. With the existing landscape of mountains, forests, and vast coastlines, they were definitely challenged. Survival meant adapting to this new environment and learning to exploit the marine resources along the coast and the terrestrial flora and fauna of the interior.

Their tools were crafted from the materials at hand: stone, bone, and shell. These artifacts have been unearthed in archaeological sites across Hispaniola and provide an incredible glimpse into the lives of these early people. They were hunters and gatherers. This means they lived in small, mobile groups and were deeply attuned to the rhythms of the seasons and the availability of resources.

As these peoples returned to Hispaniola more often and began to settle, they evolved into more complex cultures. The introduction of agriculture was a big turning point, allowing these hunter-gatherers to shift from nomadic lifestyles to more settled forms of existence. The cultivation of crops such as cassava would have transformed their relationship with the land, leading to more permanent settlements and the development of new social structures.

This gradual shift set the stage for the permanent arrival of the Taíno people. The Taíno people are considered the first official inhabitants of the island of Hispaniola. While their ancestors had been traveling the islands for some time, their arrival marked a significant development in the island's pre-Columbian history.

The movement of these people was not an isolated event but part of a larger pattern of migration and cultural exchange in the pre-Columbian Caribbean. These migrations were driven by various factors, including environmental changes, social dynamics, and the inherent human drive to explore and expand.

Early Societies and Patterns of Settlement

Before the Taíno and Caribs, whose stories are central to the pre-Columbian history of the Caribbean, earlier waves of migration and limited settlement shaped the initial human landscape of Hispaniola.

The earliest known inhabitants of Hispaniola (in what would become Haiti) were the Archaic people, often referred to as the Ciboney and Guanahatabey. These groups were primarily hunter-gatherers, adapting to the diverse environments of the island. Their presence, dating back several millennia, sets the scene for understanding the island's ancient human activity. The Ciboney were skilled at exploiting the coastal resources, fishing, and hunting small game. They were also proficient foragers, gathering fruits, roots, and nuts from the lush Caribbean forests.

Archaeological evidence of these early societies includes rudimentary tools made from stone, bone, and shell, indicating a lifestyle deeply intertwined with the natural landscape. Their settlements were likely temporary and small-scale, reflecting a nomadic or semi-nomadic lifestyle. These early inhabitants left a sparse but intriguing archaeological record, providing glimpses into their way of life.

The transition from nomadic to more settled ways of life was a gradual process. Changes in the availability of resources, climatic changes, and interactions with neighboring islands and peoples allowed for new ways to live and survive. Settlements started to grow and complexity, and the relationship with the environment became more nuanced. Agriculture began to complement hunting and gathering, leading to changes in social organization and resource management.

These initial patterns of settlement and land use laid the groundwork for the advanced societies of the Taíno and Caribs, who would later dominate the cultural landscape of the Caribbean.

Human Impact on the Environment

The early inhabitants of Hispaniola interacted with their environment in largely sustainable ways. Their agricultural practices, such as slash-and-burn, were adapted to the island's ecological conditions. While these practices altered the landscape, they were done on a scale and in a manner that allowed for ecological recovery.

However, these societies did impact their environment, and over time, these impacts became more pronounced. Deforestation for agriculture and settlement expansion began to alter the landscape. The introduction of new agricultural techniques and crops by migrating groups, especially the Taíno, led to more intensive land use and, consequently, more significant environmental changes.

Transition to the Taíno Era

As we delve deeper into the environmental narrative of pre-Columbian Hispaniola, we approach the threshold of the Taíno era. The Taíno, with their advanced agricultural practices and societal structures, represented a significant evolution in the human-environment interaction on the island. They cultivated the land more intensively and managed resources in ways that reflected an understanding of the island and a growing impact on its ecosystems.

The Taíno era, which we will explore in greater detail in the next chapter, marks a period of increased human influence on Hispaniola.

Their arrival and expansion on the island were not isolated developments but part of a broader narrative of human adaptation and environmental interaction. This period set the stage for the profound transformations that would follow with the arrival of Europeans, reshaping not just the cultural and social landscape of Hispaniola but its environment.

Chapter 2 – The Taínos and Caribs (Kalinago) – Indigenous Civilizations

In this chapter, we delve into the lives and legacies of the Taínos and Caribs, the indigenous peoples whose civilizations flourished in the Caribbean before the transformative wave of European contact. We explore the intricate societal structures, daily practices, and enduring cultural influences of these groups, shedding light on their significant but often underrepresented roles in shaping the region's history and identity.

As we navigate through the complexities of their societies, we will move beyond the simplistic narratives often found in historical accounts. This exploration illuminates their contributions to the Caribbean's cultural history and sets the stage for understanding the profound changes that ensued with the arrival of Europeans, marking a pivotal moment in the region's history.

Social Structure and Daily Life of the Taínos

In the landscapes of pre-Columbian Hispaniola and the wider Caribbean, the Taíno civilization flourished. The first part of our exploration into the Taíno civilization focuses on understanding their social hierarchy, which was pivotal in maintaining the order and function of their communities.

Caciques: Leaders of the Taíno Society

At the apex of Taíno society were the caciques, or chiefs, who wielded considerable influence and power. These leaders were not merely administrative heads; they were integral to the spiritual and cultural fabric of the community. Caciques were often chosen based on lineage, with the role frequently passing down through families. In some cases, however, they were selected for their skills, wisdom, or bravery.

The cacique's responsibilities were extensive. They oversaw the distribution of resources and judgment of disputes and made critical decisions regarding the community's welfare. In many respects, caciques were seen as paternal figures, ensuring the well-being of their people. They also played a significant role in religious ceremonies, acting as intermediaries between the Taíno people and the spiritual realm.

Nitaínos: The Nobles

Below the cacique were the nitaínos, the noble class. These individuals were typically close relatives of the cacique and held various responsibilities in the community. They were often warriors, religious leaders, and advisors to the cacique. The nitaínos also played crucial roles in organizing community work, such as agricultural activities and construction projects, ensuring that these vital tasks were carried out effectively.

Naborias: The Commoners

The backbone of Taíno society was formed by the naborias, or commoners. This group comprised most of the population and was responsible for the day-to-day activities that sustained the community. Their roles were diverse, including farming, fishing, crafting, and building. Despite their lower status in the social hierarchy, naborias were essential to the community's survival and prosperity.

Behiques: Shamans and Healers

A unique aspect of Taíno society was the role of behiques, or shamans. These individuals were revered for their knowledge of spiritual matters and medicinal practices and as the keepers of folklore and traditions. Behiques were often consulted for their wisdom and played a pivotal role in religious ceremonies and healing practices.

Understanding the hierarchical structure of Taíno society is key to comprehending their way of life, governance, and cultural practices. This system facilitated effective resource management, social cohesion, and a strong sense of community. As we delve deeper into the daily life of the Taíno in the next segment, we will explore how this social structure influenced their agricultural practices, housing, and cultural activities, providing a comprehensive picture of their everyday existence.

Daily Life and Community Practices in Taíno Society

Agriculture and Food

Agriculture was the cornerstone of Taíno daily life. The Taíno practiced a form of shifting cultivation, primarily growing cassava, a staple in their diet. Cassava was processed into various forms, including bread and a fermented drink. Maize, beans, squash, and a variety of fruits complemented their diet. This agricultural abundance supported relatively dense populations, especially in fertile regions.

Fishing supplemented their agricultural diet. Coastal communities were adept at deep-sea fishing, while riverine communities focused on freshwater species. The Taíno built canoes, some large enough to carry several people, for fishing and transportation purposes.

Housing and Village Structure

The Taíno lived in yucayeques, villages typically centered around a batey, a plaza used for various community activities, including ceremonies and the ball game known as batu. Their houses, called bohíos, were circular, made from wood, and thatched with palm leaves. Larger structures, known as caneyes, housed the cacique and served as communal spaces for meetings or gatherings.

Social and Cultural Practices

Social life in Taíno communities was rich and communal. The batey was not just a physical space but a symbol of community life. It hosted dances, religious ceremonies, and ball games, which were both recreational and had ceremonial significance.

Artistic expression was evident in pottery, weaving, and carvings. The Taíno also engaged in body art, including painting and tattooing, which often had social or religious meanings. Music and dance were integral to their cultural practices, with drums, flutes, and maracas commonly used in various ceremonies.

Religious Beliefs and Ceremonies

Taíno spirituality was deeply connected to nature, with a pantheon of gods (zemis) governing various aspects of the natural world and daily life. The Taíno believed in the afterlife and practiced ancestor worship. Religious ceremonies often involved offerings to zemis and included the use of cohoba, a hallucinogenic substance, particularly in ceremonies led by the behiques.

Craftsmanship and Trade

The Taíno were skilled craftsmen, known for their pottery, basketry, and woodworking. They traded these goods, along with agricultural products, with neighboring islands, indicating a network of regional interactions and cultural exchange.

The Taíno Influence on Caribbean Culture

Linguistic Contributions

One of the most visible legacies of the Taíno is found in language. Numerous Taíno words have been integrated into English, Spanish, other languages spoken in the Caribbean, and the global lexicon. Words such as "hurricane" (originally *hurakán*), "hammock" (*hamaka*), "canoe" (*kanawa*), "barbecue" (from *barbecoa*) and "tobacco" (*tabako*) are all derived from the Taíno language, showcasing their impact on the vocabulary used to describe the Caribbean's natural environment and indigenous technologies.

Agricultural Practices

The agricultural methods of the Taíno, particularly their techniques for cultivating cassava, have persisted over centuries. The production of cassava bread, a staple in their diet, continues in various forms across the Caribbean. This enduring agricultural practice is not just a method of food production but a living link to the Taínos' culinary heritage.

Artistic and Cultural Expressions

The artistic expressions of the Taíno, especially their pottery and carvings, have influenced Caribbean art forms. The symbolic motifs found in Taíno art continue to inspire contemporary artists in the region, reflecting a deep connection to this indigenous heritage. Additionally, Taíno musical instruments and rhythms have contributed to Caribbean music.

Spiritual Beliefs and Rituals

Elements of Taíno spirituality, with its deep connection to nature and the cosmos, have been woven into the religious tapestry of the Caribbean. Certain beliefs and rituals have blended with African and European practices, creating unique syncretic religions. The reverence for natural elements and ancestral spirits seen in some Caribbean religious practices can be traced back to Taíno spiritual beliefs.

Medicinal Knowledge

The Taínos' use of medicinal plants and natural remedies has had a lasting impact on traditional Caribbean medicine. Many of the herbal treatments and natural healing practices used in the region today have roots in Taíno knowledge passed down through generations.

Environmental Management

The Taínos' relationship with their environment, characterized by a deep understanding of and respect for nature, provides a model for contemporary environmental management in the Caribbean. Their sustainable practices and balanced approach to resource utilization offer valuable lessons in an age of environmental challenges.

As we conclude our exploration of the Taínos' cultural contributions, it becomes evident that their legacy is woven into the fabric of Caribbean life. The next segment will shift focus to the Caribs, another indigenous group that played a significant role in the region. We will explore common misconceptions about the Caribs, aiming to provide a clearer understanding of their culture and impact on Caribbean history.

Understanding the Caribs

It's essential to recognize the Caribs, now known as the Kalinago, and their profound influence on the Caribbean's cultural and historical landscape. The Kalinago were among the indigenous peoples who played a pivotal role in shaping the early history of the island of Hispaniola, including that of the Dominican Republic. Despite not settling there permanently, they raided often and were an important part of the lives of the early peoples.

Their presence, traditions, and interactions with other indigenous groups and later European settlers constitute a significant chapter in the island's history. Understanding the Kalinago's way of life, social structure, and the challenges they faced provides insight into the pre-Columbian era and helps us appreciate the complex interplay of cultures that defines the Caribbean's history.

Societal Structure and Daily Life of the Caribs

Carib society, like the Taíno, was organized hierarchically but with distinct features. Leadership was typically vested in a cacique. However, Carib caciques often held their positions based more on merit, particularly prowess in warfare and navigation, than hereditary right.

Beneath the cacique was a class of elders and warriors who played significant roles in decision-making, especially in matters of war and external relations. Unlike the Taíno, the Caribs were known for their seafaring capabilities, and those skilled in navigation and raiding held high status within their society.

Women in Carib society had distinct roles, often involved in agricultural practices and domestic activities. They also held certain influential positions, particularly in spiritual and medicinal practices.

Daily Life

The daily life of the Caribs was significantly influenced by their environment, with a strong emphasis on maritime activities. They were adept at building and navigating canoes, which they used for fishing, transportation, and raids on neighboring islands. Fishing was a major part of their diet, supplemented by agriculture, with crops like cassava, maize, and sweet potatoes.

Carib settlements were generally located along coastlines or riverbanks, taking advantage of the maritime resources. Their houses, though similar in construction to the Taíno bohíos, were easier to assemble and disassemble, reflecting their more mobile lifestyle.

Cultural Practices

Cultural practices among the Caribs were diverse, with variations across different islands. They were known for their elaborate body art, including painting and tattooing, which held social and spiritual significance. Their craftsmanship in pottery, basket weaving, and canoe building was highly developed and integral to their daily life.

Spiritual beliefs in Carib society were deeply connected to nature and ancestor worship. Shamanic practices and rituals played a crucial role, with spiritual leaders often mediating between the community and the spiritual world.

Maritime Skills and Warfare

The Caribs' maritime skills were not just for sustenance but also formed a key aspect of their identity. Their prowess in building canoes and navigating the Caribbean waters set them apart from other indigenous groups. Additionally, their skills in warfare, particularly naval engagements, were renowned. They engaged in raids for resources, territory, and sometimes as part of their ritual practices.

Dispelling Common Misconceptions

The Caribs are a group often shrouded in myth and misconception. It is crucial to separate fact from fiction to gain a true understanding of their role in Caribbean history. This segment aims to demystify the Caribs, often portrayed inaccurately in popular narratives and historical accounts.

Misconception 1: The Caribs as Ferocious Cannibals

One of the most persistent misconceptions about the Caribs is that they were fierce cannibals, a stereotype perpetuated by early European colonizers. Modern research, however, suggests that this image was likely exaggerated and used as a justification for the colonization and enslavement of the Carib people. While there might have been ritualistic practices involving human remains, the extent of the Caribs' cannibalism has been significantly overstated in historical records.

Misconception 2: The Caribs as Nomadic Raiders

Another common portrayal is that the Caribs were nomadic raiders constantly at war with neighboring tribes, particularly the Taínos. While the Caribs were indeed skilled warriors and navigators who occasionally engaged in conflicts, they also had established settlements and complex societal structures. Their interactions with other indigenous groups were multifaceted, including trade and cultural exchange, not solely defined by conflict.

Misconception 3: The Caribs' Disappearance Post-European Contact

It is often mistakenly believed that the Caribs vanished or were entirely wiped out following European colonization. In reality, while they suffered greatly due to diseases, enslavement, and warfare, Carib communities survived and adapted. Today, their descendants can be found in parts of the Caribbean, maintaining their cultural heritage and identity.

Misconception 4: Homogeneity of the Carib Culture

There is a tendency to view the Caribs as a homogeneous group with a uniform culture. In truth, the Caribs were diverse, with variations in language, customs, and social structures across different islands and regions. This diversity is essential in understanding the broad spectrum of Carib societies and their adaptability to various environments.

Misconception 5: Limited Carib Influence on Modern Caribbean Culture

Often overshadowed by the Taínos, the Caribs' influence on contemporary Caribbean culture is sometimes underestimated. However, their contributions, particularly in terms of maritime technology, agricultural practices, and linguistic elements, have left a lasting impact on the region.

As we dispel these misconceptions, the true picture of the Caribs begins to emerge—one of a resilient, adaptable, and complex society that played a crucial role in the pre-Columbian Caribbean. Their story is not one of a mysterious, vanished tribe but of a people who navigated the challenges of their time and left a legacy.

The Caribs' Contributions to Modern Caribbean Culture

The Caribs' exceptional skills in canoe building and navigation stand out as a remarkable contribution to the Caribbean's maritime heritage. Their canoes, known for their durability and design, were crucial for fishing, trade, and exploration across the Caribbean Sea. The Carib approach to seafaring not only facilitated their survival and dominance in the region but also influenced maritime practices in the Caribbean, including boat-building techniques still observed in some areas today.

Linguistic Influence

The Carib language, though less integrated into modern languages compared to Taíno, has left its mark in the Caribbean. Several place names across the region have origins in the Carib language, reflecting its historical presence and impact. Additionally, the Carib language has influenced the lexicon of Caribbean Creole languages, contributing to the linguistic diversity of the region.

Cultural Practices and Art

Carib cultural practices, particularly their art and craftsmanship, have a lasting presence in the Caribbean. Their intricate basketry, pottery, and woodcarvings are not only historical artifacts but also serve as inspiration for contemporary Caribbean artisans. The Carib tradition of storytelling and oral history has also played a role in shaping the region's rich narrative tradition.

Spiritual and Medicinal Legacy

Spiritually, the Caribs' reverence for nature and their shamanistic practices have influenced Caribbean folk traditions and beliefs. Their understanding of medicinal plants and natural remedies has been passed down through generations, contributing to the traditional healing practices still used in some Caribbean communities.

Adaptation and Resilience

Perhaps one of the most significant legacies of the Caribs is their story of adaptation and resilience. Despite facing significant challenges from European colonization and other threats, the Caribs' ability to adapt and survive echoes in the resilience seen in Caribbean societies today. This legacy is a testament to their strength and enduring presence in the region.

Facing a New Horizon

As we look back at the Taíno and Carib civilizations, their story is not just one of pre-Columbian history but also their role in shaping the modern Caribbean identity. Their legacy, surviving through centuries of change and challenge, serves as a bridge connecting the past to the present.

The arrival of Europeans marked a significant turning point for the Taínos and Caribs. It introduced a period of immense challenge and transformation, reshaping the Caribbean's human and ecological landscapes. Yet, the persistence of Taíno influences in modern culture is a testament to their ability to adapt and endure.

This period of contact and conquest did not erase the indigenous presence; rather, it created a complex cultural mosaic. The Taínos and Caribs, through their interactions with Europeans, left an indelible mark on the cultural and historical trajectory of the Caribbean.

Chapter 3 – Encounter and Conquest

Our exploration of the encounter and conquest phase begins with Christopher Columbus's first voyage across the Atlantic in 1492. This journey, funded by the Spanish monarchy, aimed to discover a westward sea route to Asia but instead led to the momentous first contact with the Caribbean islands and their inhabitants.

Columbus, an Italian explorer, set sail from Spain with three ships: the Niña, the Pinta, and the Santa María. After a challenging journey across the Atlantic, Columbus and his crew first sighted land in what is now known as the Bahamas. This event marked the beginning of European exploration in the Americas.

Columbus's first encounter was with the Taíno people, who inhabited the islands of the Caribbean. These initial interactions were marked by a mixture of curiosity and misunderstanding. Columbus, believing he had reached the outskirts of Asia, was keen on establishing profitable trade relations and finding gold. The Taínos, encountering Europeans for the first time, exhibited a combination of hospitality and caution.

Columbus's Assessment and Actions

Columbus's observations of the Taíno people and their environment were documented with a sense of wonder and opportunism. He noted the Taínos' gold ornaments and the potential for exploiting the islands' resources. Columbus also took several Taíno individuals aboard his ships, intending to bring them back to Spain as evidence of his discoveries.

Columbus returned to Spain with tales of his discoveries, setting the stage for further exploration and eventual colonization of the Caribbean. The idea of more permanent settlements didn't come until Columbus's subsequent voyages. These developments marked the beginning of a new era in the region, drastically altering the course of its history and that of its indigenous inhabitants.

Columbus's Subsequent Voyages and Escalating Tensions

Columbus's second voyage in 1493 marked a significant escalation from exploration to colonization. With a fleet of seventeen ships and around 1,200 men, Columbus returned to the Caribbean, this time with the explicit intent of establishing Spanish presence and dominance. This expedition led to the discovery of several new islands and initiated the process of mapping the Caribbean region.

During these voyages, Columbus and his crew encountered other indigenous groups besides the Taínos, such as the Caribs. These encounters varied in nature but often involved conflict and violence, as Columbus sought to subjugate the indigenous populations and claim territories for Spain.

Columbus's actions during these voyages have been a subject of controversy and debate. His policies and methods, including forced labor, harsh treatment of the indigenous populations, and the quest for gold, set a precedent for subsequent colonizers in the region. Columbus's legacy is thus intertwined with the early history of European colonization in the Americas, marked by both discovery and exploitation.

Establishment of La Navidad and La Isabela

One of Columbus's key actions during his second voyage was establishing the settlement of La Navidad on Hispaniola, on the site of a shipwreck from his first voyage. However, La Navidad was short-lived, as tensions with local Taíno communities led to its destruction. Subsequently, Columbus established La Isabela in 1494, which became the first permanent European settlement in the Americas but faced numerous challenges, including resistance from the Taíno people.

Concepción de la Vega

Concepción de la Vega, located in the fertile Cibao Valley, was founded by Columbus during his second voyage. Its strategic position made it a hub for expeditions into the interior of Hispaniola and a center for the burgeoning Spanish colonial administration. The city was laid out in a grid pattern, typical of Spanish colonial urban design, and rapidly developed into a flourishing community.

The settlement's significance was largely due to its proximity to gold mines, which were among the first to be exploited by the Spanish in the New World. The economic activities in and around Concepción de la Vega were pivotal in sustaining the Spanish colonial endeavors during the early years of occupation. The city became a bustling center of commerce, attracting settlers, adventurers, and missionaries.

Concepción de la Vega also played a critical role in the cultural and social dynamics of early colonial Hispaniola. It was a site where diverse cultures intersected—European settlers, indigenous Taíno communities, and, later, African slaves. The city thus became a melting pot of cultural exchanges, conflicts, and syntheses that would shape the character of the region.

However, Concepción de la Vega's prosperity was short-lived. The city suffered a significant blow during a devastating earthquake in 1562, leading to its eventual abandonment. The ruins of the old city, particularly the remains of the Basilica of Santa María, stand today as a testament to its historical significance.

Establishing Initial European Settlements

These early European settlements served as strategic points for further colonial expansion in the Caribbean and the Americas. They became centers from which the Spanish launched explorations, sought resources, and enforced their authority over the indigenous peoples. The settlements also played a role in establishing the patterns of European colonization, including the encomienda system, which had profound implications for the indigenous population.

Challenges and Early Conflicts

The establishment of these settlements was not without challenges. The Europeans faced difficulties in adapting to the new environment, leading to struggles with food supply and disease. Add in the resistance from the indigenous peoples (although initially limited), and the impacts of colonization became more apparent.

The early European settlements in the Caribbean were more than mere footholds in the New World. They were the starting points of a new era in the region, one that would lead to significant cultural and demographic shifts. These settlements laid the groundwork for the complex colonial dynamics that would dominate the Caribbean for centuries to come.

The Dynamics of Early European Settlements

As the Europeans established a firmer foothold in the Caribbean, they also expanded and changed the nature of their settlements. Santo Domingo, on Hispaniola, grew in importance as a colonial hub. Driven by the allure of gold and other resources, they began to exploit the land and its people. The initial period of cooperation and trade with the Taínos gradually gave way to more exploitative and hostile relationships. This exploitation was not limited to mining; it extended to agriculture, with the introduction of new crops and farming methods.

The European settlements became centers of cultural and social change. While they introduced new technologies and ideas, they also disrupted the existing social and cultural fabric of the indigenous communities. The impact was not solely negative. Instances of cultural exchange and intermarriage led to the emergence of a mixed population with blended customs and traditions.

Santo Domingo Historic Center, Dominican Republic.
By neufal54; Free to use: https://pixabay.com/service/license-summary/;
https://pixabay.com/fr/photos/saint-domingue-centre-historique-2681745/

The Impact of Conquest on Indigenous Societies

The most immediate and devastating impact of European arrival was the dramatic decline in the indigenous population. This decline was caused by several factors, including diseases brought by Europeans, such as smallpox, against which the Taínos and Caribs had no immunity. Additionally, the harsh labor conditions, warfare, and disruption of traditional ways of life contributed significantly to the population decrease.

The Spanish encomienda system, where indigenous peoples were essentially enslaved and forced to labor in mines, plantations, and other enterprises, led to exploitation and abuse, further exacerbating the decline in indigenous populations. The Taínos, known for their agricultural skills, were particularly affected, as they were forced to adapt to the demanding labor requirements of the colonizers.

The arrival of Europeans and their conquest led to the disintegration of the traditional social and cultural structures of the Taínos and Caribs. Indigenous religions, customs, and practices were suppressed or lost, as European cultural norms and Christianity were imposed. This cultural imposition was not only a matter of religion and customs but also involved the restructuring of indigenous governance and community organization.

Resistance and Adaptation

Despite the overwhelming challenges, indigenous communities resisted the European conquest in various ways. This resistance included armed rebellions, such as the Taíno uprising led by Enriquillo. Some indigenous communities fled to remote areas to escape European control, while others adapted by incorporating aspects of European culture into their own.

Enriquillo was a Taíno cacique (chief) who had initially been raised in a Franciscan monastery and was well-versed in Spanish ways and language. Enriquillo became increasingly disenchanted with the brutal treatment of his people, perhaps because he was exposed to it at an early age.

Around 1519, Enriquillo led a rebellion that would last for over a decade. The rebellion was sparked by a series of injustices and abuses inflicted upon the Taíno by the Spanish, including the encomienda system. He and his followers retreated to the Bahoruco Mountains, using the rugged terrain to their advantage. From this stronghold, they conducted guerrilla warfare against the Spanish, attacking colonial settlements and disrupting their operations. Enriquillo's rebellion was notable for its organization, duration, and the significant challenge it posed to Spanish authority.

The rebellion eventually led the Spanish to negotiate with Enriquillo, a remarkable event given the colonial attitudes of the time. In 1533, a peace treaty granted Enriquillo and his followers land and freedoms that were unprecedented for indigenous people under Spanish rule. This treaty was a significant acknowledgment of the legitimacy of the Taíno resistance.

Legacy of Enriquillo's Rebellion

The rebellion led by Enriquillo is more than a historical footnote; it represents a poignant example of indigenous resistance and agency in the face of colonial oppression. It highlights the complexities of early colonial interactions and the capacity of indigenous leaders to challenge and negotiate with European powers.

Enriquillo's rebellion stands as a testament to the resilience of the Taíno people and has become a symbol of resistance and pride in Dominican and Caribbean history. This event underscores the struggles and strength of the Taíno, offering a deeper understanding of the indigenous perspective during a transformative and tumultuous period in Hispaniola's history.

Long-term Effects on Indigenous Societies

The long-term effects of the European conquest on indigenous societies were profound. The demographic collapse led to significant changes in the ethnic composition of the Caribbean, with the later introduction of African slaves and the emergence of mixed-race populations. Indigenous knowledge, languages, and practices were significantly diminished, though not entirely erased.

Cultural Endurance in the Face of Adversity

Despite the severe population decline and cultural disruptions, some indigenous communities survived, retreating to remote areas or blending into the emerging colonial societies. These survivors continued to practice elements of their traditional culture, albeit often in secrecy or blended with European and African influences. Over generations, this resilience ensured that aspects of indigenous heritage, from agricultural techniques to linguistic traces, persisted.

Shaping the Future Colonial Landscape

The remnants of indigenous practices and knowledge would subtly influence the unfolding colonial era. As the Caribbean entered a period dominated by the sugar boom, the agricultural knowledge and environmental management practices of the Taínos and Caribs would echo in the new economic landscape. The sugar plantations, which would come to define much of the Caribbean's colonial economy, were built on land once cultivated by these indigenous peoples.

The shift to a plantation-dominated economy was a significant departure from the past, yet it was built upon the layered history of the region, a history marked by resilience, adaptation, and cultural amalgamation. This historical context is vital for understanding the dramatic transformations during the colonial period. The legacy of the Taínos and Caribs, though often overshadowed, continued to echo as the Caribbean navigated the complexities of colonial rule and economic expansion.

Chapter 4 – Colonial Era and the Sugar Boom

The Caribbean, under European colonial rule, began a transformation that reshaped its society and economy. European countries established strong governance systems to control their new territories. These administrations mirrored European models and were responsible for resource management, trade, and law and order.

Emergence of Social Hierarchies

Colonial society in the Caribbean was characterized by a distinct social hierarchy. Europeans, particularly those from ruling nations, occupied the top tier, wielding power and wealth. Below them were mixed-race individuals and freed African slaves, who occupied an intermediate social status. At the bottom were the enslaved Africans, who formed the backbone of the plantation economy but had the least social standing.

Despite the rigid social structure, there was a degree of cultural blending. European, African, and surviving indigenous influences began to merge, creating a unique Caribbean culture. This syncretism was evident in language, food, music, and religious practices, reflecting the diverse origins of the Caribbean population.

Expansion and Evolution of Colonial Economies

Continuing our exploration of the early colonial era in the Caribbean, we focus on the expansion and evolution of colonial economies. This period saw significant developments in the region's economic structures, laying the groundwork for the later sugar boom.

Initially, the colonial economy focused on subsistence farming and using natural resources like timber and minerals. Besides agriculture, they engaged in logging, fishing, and small-scale manufacturing. European colonists experimented with different crops and goods to determine what was most profitable in the new environment.

However, the fertility of the Caribbean lands soon led to an agricultural shift toward cash crops. Tobacco and cotton were among the first to be cultivated on a large scale for export to Europe. This marked the beginning of significant changes in the Caribbean's economic landscape.

Trade played a crucial role in the growth of colonial economies. The Caribbean became a hub for international trade, with goods flowing in from Europe, Africa, and the Americas. Colonies traded sugar, rum, tobacco, and other products for European manufactured goods, African slaves, and other commodities. Port cities grew rapidly, becoming vital centers of economic activity.

Over time, many Caribbean colonies began to focus on a single main crop or product, a system known as monoculture. This shift was driven by the high demand and profits from certain crops in European markets. Monoculture made the colonies economically efficient but also more dependent on a single commodity, making them vulnerable to market changes.

The economic changes brought by colonization had significant impacts on the local populations and environments. The focus on cash crops led to the clearing of large areas of land, changing the landscape. Indigenous peoples and smaller farmers often lost their land to large plantations.

Role of European Companies and Investors

European companies and investors played a significant role in the colonial economies. Companies like the British East India Company and the Dutch West India Company were granted monopolies and rights to trade in certain areas. These companies invested in plantations, trade, and infrastructure, contributing to the economic development of the colonies.

The Economic Mechanisms and International Trade of the Sugar Industry

The sugar industry in the Caribbean during the colonial era was not just a local economic activity; it was deeply connected to global trade and European economic policies. Understanding these economic mechanisms provides insight into the vast impact of sugar on the Caribbean and beyond.

European powers during the colonial era followed mercantilist policies. These policies aimed to strengthen national economies by maximizing exports and minimizing imports. The Caribbean sugar industry was integral to this strategy. European countries viewed their colonies as sources of valuable commodities, like sugar, which they could sell in international markets.

The sugar industry was a crucial part of the triangular trade system. This system involved shipping goods from Europe to Africa, where they were exchanged for enslaved people. These enslaved Africans were then transported to the Caribbean and the Americas and sold to work in plantations. The final leg of the triangle involved shipping sugar and other plantation products back to Europe.

The focus on sugar production led to a monocultural economy, While this focus brought wealth, the Caribbean economies' dependence on a single commodity made them vulnerable to market fluctuations. The focus on the sugar industry also shifted land use and labor patterns. Land previously used for food crops or left in its natural state was converted into sugar plantations. This change had far-reaching implications, including food shortages and the need to import basic necessities.

The success of sugar plantations required significant investment. Plantation owners and European investors poured money into developing plantation infrastructure, including mills, boiling houses, and transportation systems. Ports and shipping facilities were also expanded to handle the large volumes of sugar being exported.

Legacy of the Sugar Economy

The sugar economy left a legacy in the Caribbean. It established the region as a key player in global trade but also entrenched systems of slavery and social inequality. The wealth generated from sugar production was unevenly distributed, with plantation owners and European powers benefiting the most.

The economic mechanisms and international trade aspects of the sugar industry were fundamental to the colonial era in the Caribbean. They not only shaped the region's economy but also had profound effects on its society, environment, and global connections.

The Impact of the Sugar Industry on African Slavery

As mentioned, the demand for labor on the vast sugar plantations was a key driver of the transatlantic slave trade. European colonists sought a workforce capable of enduring the grueling conditions of sugar production. This demand led to the forcible transportation of millions of Africans across the Atlantic Ocean, in a journey marked by brutality and suffering known as the Middle Passage.

Life for enslaved Africans on sugar plantations was characterized by extreme hardship. The work was backbreaking and relentless, with long hours spent in the fields under the scorching sun. Tasks included planting, tending, and harvesting sugar cane, followed by processing it in mills. Many slaves suffered from malnutrition, diseases, and injuries due to the harsh working and living conditions.

Despite the hardships, enslaved Africans were essential to the sugar industry. They were involved in every aspect of sugar production, from the initial planting to the final processing stages. Their knowledge, skills, and labor were crucial, though often unacknowledged, in making the Caribbean sugar plantations some of the most profitable enterprises for European colonizers.

Resistance and Cultural Resilience

Amidst the oppression, enslaved Africans found ways to resist and retain their dignity. Acts of resistance ranged from subtle forms of defiance, like work slowdowns, to outright rebellion and uprisings. These acts of resistance were dangerous but underscored the Africans' unyielding spirit and desire for freedom.

Enslaved Africans also managed to preserve elements of their diverse cultural heritage. They maintained traditional African languages, religious beliefs, music, and dance, which they passed down through generations. This cultural legacy significantly influenced the development of a unique Afro-Caribbean culture.

1521 Santo Domingo Slave Revolt

The 1521 Santo Domingo Slave Revolt stands as one of the earliest recorded slave uprisings in the New World, a significant event that underscores the resistance of African slaves against the brutalities of the transatlantic slave trade and colonial exploitation.

The uprising in 1521 was led by enslaved Africans who had been forced into labor in the sugar plantations and gold mines around Santo Domingo, the capital of the Spanish colony. Discontent had been brewing due to the unbearable working conditions and the cruelty of the overseers. The rebels planned and executed a coordinated uprising, showcasing remarkable courage and a desire for freedom.

The Spanish colonial authorities responded with swift and brutal force to suppress the revolt. The uprising was quelled, and those who participated were subject to severe punishment. The rebellion's suppression demonstrated the colonial regime's determination to maintain the slave system and its economic benefits at any cost.

Though not successful in achieving immediate freedom for its participants, the 1521 Santo Domingo Slave Revolt is historically significant for several reasons. It highlighted the inherent resistance of the enslaved Africans to their subjugation and laid the groundwork for future slave rebellions in the Caribbean and the Americas. The revolt also prompted the Spanish authorities to reconsider their strategies for controlling and managing enslaved populations.

The 1521 Santo Domingo Slave Revolt is a poignant reminder of the struggles and resistance of African slaves in the early colonial period. It serves as an important testament to the fight against oppression and the human spirit's quest for freedom and dignity. This event adds a critical dimension to understanding the complex social and economic dynamics of early colonial Hispaniola.

The Road to Abolition

The abolitionist movement, which gained momentum in the late eighteenth and early nineteenth centuries, was a response to the moral and ethical concerns regarding slavery. This movement, combined with slave uprisings and economic factors, gradually led to the abolition of slavery. Emancipation was a turning point, yet it presented new challenges for the formerly enslaved and the plantation economies.

Post-emancipation, freed slaves faced the challenge of integrating into societies that had long viewed them as property. Many remained in rural areas, working as laborers on plantations, while others moved to urban centers in search of new opportunities. The end of slavery marked the beginning of a new chapter in Caribbean history, characterized by struggles for civil rights, economic independence, and cultural recognition.

The relationship between African slavery and the sugar industry was complex, leaving a legacy that continued to influence Caribbean society long after the abolition of slavery. Understanding this relationship is crucial to comprehending the historical dynamics of the region and the persistent challenges and contributions of its Afro-descendant population.

Social Hierarchies and Race Relations in the Colonial Caribbean

In the Caribbean's colonial era, dominated by the sugar industry, a complex social structure emerged. This structure was deeply rooted in race, class, and economic power, significantly impacting the lives and interactions of people in the region.

The social hierarchy was topped by Europeans, including British, French, Spanish, and Dutch colonists. They held the most power, owning the plantations, land, and enslaved people. As the ruling class, they controlled the economy, made laws, and governed the colonies. Their wealth and status afforded them a lifestyle of privilege and influence, far removed from the hardships of plantation life.

Middle Social Tiers: Free People of Mixed Heritage and Freed Slaves

Beneath the Europeans were free people of mixed heritage, often referred to as mulattos. These individuals, born from European and African unions, occupied a unique position in society. They were freer than enslaved Africans but faced discrimination and limitations due to their mixed race. Many in this group worked as skilled artisans, small business owners, or intermediate supervisors on plantations. Some owned property and even slaves, navigating a complex social landscape between freedom and the constraints of racial prejudice.

Freed slaves, or manumitted individuals, also formed part of this intermediate social tier. Gaining freedom through various means, such as purchase, emancipation, or as a reward for service, these individuals strived to build lives in a society that still viewed them through the lens of their former enslaved status. Their experiences and social positions varied, with some achieving economic success and others struggling to escape the shadow of slavery.

Enslaved Africans: The Foundation of the Plantation Economy

The base of the social pyramid was comprised of enslaved Africans, who endured the harshest conditions. Their lives were defined by labor on the sugar plantations, where they worked long, grueling hours with little respite. The brutality of slavery, lack of rights, and harsh punishments were daily realities. Despite this, enslaved Africans maintained a resilient spirit, preserving elements of their diverse cultural heritages and forging new cultural identities in the Caribbean.

Daily Life and Cultural Interactions

Daily life in the colonial Caribbean was profoundly influenced by one's position in the social hierarchy. This stratification dictated the type of work individuals did, their living conditions, and the extent of their rights and freedoms. The rigid class system also shaped interactions between different groups, often leading to tensions but also facilitating cultural exchanges. The blending of European, African, and indigenous cultures gave rise to unique Caribbean traditions in music, dance, religion, and language.

The Slow Road to Social Change

The journey toward social equality was gradual and fraught with challenges. The abolition of slavery marked a turning point but did not immediately dismantle the established social hierarchies. Freed slaves and people of mixed heritage gradually gained more rights, but the road to full equality was long and arduous.

The social hierarchies established during the colonial era left a legacy in the Caribbean. Even after the colonies gained independence, these structures continued to influence the region's societal dynamics. Race, class, and heritage remained important factors in shaping identities and interactions within Caribbean societies.

Legacy of the Colonial Era in the Caribbean

The colonial era, dominated by the sugar industry, left a complex legacy in the Caribbean. It shaped the region's economic, social, and cultural landscape and set the stage for the upcoming era of piracy, smuggling, and colonial rivalry. The challenges of managing lucrative colonies in a region fraught with conflict and illicit activities would significantly influence the Caribbean's subsequent history.

As the Caribbean transitioned from structured colonial economies to an era characterized by high-seas adventure and strategic power plays, it moved into a period that is often romanticized but was fraught with danger and intrigue. The next chapter delves into the world of pirates, smugglers, and the intense rivalry between colonial powers, uncovering how these elements further shaped the Caribbean's history and identity.

Chapter 5 – Pirates, Smugglers, and Colonial Rivals

The Caribbean, in its colonial era, was not just a landscape of burgeoning plantations and European colonization. It was also a stage for a more shadowed and tumultuous narrative. This period saw the seas around Hispaniola and neighboring islands teem with pirates, clandestine trade networks thrive under the nose of Spanish rule, and European powers engage in a relentless struggle for dominance.

The age of piracy, often romanticized in tales and lore, was a reality that brought both peril and intrigue to the Caribbean waters. These pirates influenced the political and economic dynamics of the region. The waters of Hispaniola were a crucial hub in the colonial trade routes and became a focal point of their activities.

Parallel to the tales of piracy, another form of defiance took shape in the form of smuggling. As a response to the stringent trade restrictions imposed by colonial powers, particularly Spain, clandestine trade networks emerged. These illicit activities not only fueled local economies but also slowly chipped away at the Spanish monopoly, setting a precedent for future economic transformations.

Amidst these narratives of piracy and smuggling, a grander and more complex political drama unfolded. The contest for control of Hispaniola became a microcosm of the larger struggle among European powers for supremacy in the New World. This contest, marked by diplomatic maneuvers, military confrontations, and strategic alliances, shaped the course of the island's history and had profound implications for the future of the Caribbean.

Together, these elements of piracy, smuggling, and colonial rivalry composed a vibrant and tumultuous chapter in the history of the Caribbean. They depict a period marked by adventure and danger but also significant shifts in power and the gradual emergence of new socio-political landscapes.

The Rise of Piracy in the Caribbean and Early Impact on Hispaniola

In the late sixteenth and early seventeenth centuries, the Caribbean became a hotbed for piracy. This era significantly impacted Hispaniola.

Piracy thrived in the Caribbean due to several factors. The wealth flowing through the Caribbean sea-lanes, loaded with European goods and New World treasures, presented irresistible opportunities for pirates. The political rivalries among European powers, each vying for dominance in the New World, further fueled piracy. Privateers, sanctioned by governments to raid enemy ships, often turned to piracy, lured by the promise of wealth and freedom.

Hispaniola, shared by the Spanish colony of Santo Domingo and later the French colony of Saint-Domingue, was strategically important due to its location along major trade routes. This made it a prime target for pirates seeking to intercept treasure fleets. Additionally, the island's coastline, with its many inlets and coves, offered ideal hideouts and bases for pirate operations.

Early Pirate Activities around Hispaniola

Initially, pirate activities around Hispaniola involved opportunistic attacks on passing ships, targeting vessels laden with gold, silver, and other valuable commodities. These early raids were relatively small in scale but began to disrupt the flow of wealth from the Americas to Europe. The impact of piracy on Hispaniola, especially on its local settlements and trade, was both profound and multifaceted.

The Spanish, who heavily relied on the export of goods from their New World colonies, faced significant losses as pirates frequently intercepted and looted their ships. This disruption extended beyond the mere loss of goods; it affected the entire economic structure of the island, as resources were increasingly diverted to defense rather than trade and development.

The construction of forts and naval defenses became a priority for the colonial administration. In Santo Domingo, for instance, the Spanish erected substantial fortifications, such as the Ozama Fortress, designed to protect the harbor and city against pirate raids. These defensive measures, however, required substantial investment and often strained the colony's resources. And, despite these efforts, the pirates' superior naval skills and knowledge of the local waters often gave them an advantage.

Pirate activities also impacted trade patterns, causing instability in prices and the availability of goods. The fear of piracy led to increased insurance costs for shipping, which, in turn, raised the prices of imported goods. The uncertainty and risk associated with maritime trade discouraged merchants and investors, leading to a decrease in trade volume.

Social and Cultural Effects

The constant threat of piracy also had social and cultural implications for Hispaniola. The fear of raids led to a sense of insecurity among the settlers, influencing their lifestyles and daily routines. In some areas, coastal communities were forced to relocate inland for safety, altering the demographic patterns of the island.

The presence of pirates in and around Hispaniola contributed to a unique cultural dynamic. While some pirates were feared, others were admired and even romanticized by local populations. Pirate tales and folklore became part of the island's cultural heritage, with stories of infamous pirates and daring escapades being passed down through generations.

In some cases, local populations found ways to adapt to, and even benefit from, the presence of pirates. This included engaging in illicit trade with pirates and providing them with supplies and information in exchange for a share of the plunder or protection. Such collaboration, though risky, offered an alternative economic opportunity for locals affected by the disruption of regular trade.

The impact of piracy on Hispaniola during this period was a complex interplay of economic hardship, cultural adaptation, and societal change. It highlighted the vulnerability of colonial settlements to external threats and their resilience in the face of adversity. As the era of piracy progressed, Hispaniola's strategic importance in the Caribbean would continue to make it a central player in the unfolding story of pirates, smugglers, and colonial rivals.

Tortuga: A Brief History and Its Role in Piracy

Tortuga, known as Île de la Tortue in French, is a small island in the Caribbean Sea that forms part of Haiti. Before the arrival of Europeans, the island was inhabited by the indigenous Taíno people.

The island was first claimed by Spain but was largely ignored due to its perceived lack of resources. This neglect allowed French and English buccaneers to establish a presence on Tortuga in the early 1600s. The island's natural harbors and rugged terrain made it an ideal base for these groups, who initially supplemented their income by hunting wild cattle and boars.

Transition to Piracy

Tortuga's significance in piracy began to rise as the buccaneers, joined by other adventurers and outlaws, started to engage in piracy. The island's location near the shipping lanes of the Spanish Main made it a perfect staging ground for attacks on Spanish galleons laden with treasures from the Americas. By the mid-seventeenth century, Tortuga had become a notorious pirate haven.

Tortuga's economy during this period revolved around piracy and its associated activities. The island served as a marketplace where pirates could sell their plundered goods, restock supplies, and plan future raids. The society of Tortuga was cosmopolitan and lawless, attracting individuals from various backgrounds drawn by the promise of wealth and adventure.

Eventually, the French took control of Tortuga, formalizing their rule in the mid-seventeenth century. Under French governance, the island continued to be a base for privateers, who were authorized by the government to attack enemy ships during wartime. However, the golden age of piracy gradually waned as European powers began to crack down on pirate activities in the late seventeenth and early eighteenth centuries.

Tortuga's Legacy

Tortuga's legacy in the history of piracy is enduring. The island's brief but impactful role as a pirate haven has captured the imagination of many, often romanticized in literature and popular culture. Its history provides a glimpse into the lawless and adventurous world of Caribbean piracy, offering insights into the geopolitical and economic dynamics of the colonial Caribbean.

In the broader context of Caribbean history, Tortuga stands as a testament to the era's complexity. Its story is intertwined with that of Hispaniola and the wider region, reflecting the turbulent and often violent dynamics of the time.

Famous Pirates around Hispaniola

The age of piracy in the Caribbean is marked by the exploits of several infamous pirates, many of whom had significant ties to Hispaniola. Their daring raids and legendary tales played a central role in the island's history during this tumultuous era.

Henry Morgan: A Notorious Privateer

Captain Henry Morgan, one of the most infamous figures in Caribbean piracy, often blurs the line between a privateer and a pirate. His activities, though sanctioned by the English government, were characterized by the same audacity and violence of any feared pirate of his time.

The Sack of Portobelo

In 1668, Henry Morgan set his sights on one of the most fortified Spanish settlements in the New World—Portobelo, on the coast of modern-day Panama. Portobelo was a crucial part of Spain's shipping route, where silver and gold from South America were stored before being transported to Europe. Morgan, with a fleet of ships and a band of ruthless buccaneers, launched a daring attack on the city.

The battle for Portobelo was fierce, but Morgan's strategic cunning and the firepower of his men ultimately led to the city's capture. The victory was shocking due to Portobelo's strong defenses and strategic importance. Morgan and his men looted the city, extracting a hefty ransom before withdrawing. This raid cemented Morgan's reputation as a formidable and fearless privateer.

After the sack of Portobelo, Morgan frequently used Hispaniola as a base for his operations. The island's strategic location in the heart of the Caribbean made it an ideal launching point for attacks on Spanish possessions and ships. From hidden coves along the coast of Hispaniola, Morgan planned some of his most ambitious raids, including the famous attack on Panama City in 1671.

Morgan's activities had significant implications for Hispaniola and the broader Caribbean. His use of the island as a base contributed to its reputation as a pirate haven. The constant threat of raids by Morgan and other buccaneers prompted the Spanish to strengthen their defenses in the region, diverting resources that might have been used elsewhere in their American territories.

Blackbeard: The Fearsome Pirate

Edward Teach, better known as Blackbeard, casts a long shadow over the Golden Age of Piracy. His ruthless tactics and his fearsome appearance, with fuses smoking from his beard during battles, have become the stuff of legend. His flagship, *Queen Anne's Revenge*, was a formidable presence in the Caribbean Sea, striking fear in the hearts of sailors and merchants alike.

Hispaniola and the Blockade of Charleston

While Blackbeard's activities were widespread across the Caribbean, his interactions with Hispaniola were notable. The island's strategic location made it a frequent point of interest for him, either as a hunting ground for richly laden Spanish galleons or as a place to resupply and plan further marauding activities. One of Blackbeard's most audacious exploits was the blockade of Charleston, South Carolina, in 1718.

In this bold move, Blackbeard effectively blockaded the port of Charleston, capturing and looting multiple ships. He made outrageous demands for a ransom—a chest of medicine—knowing its value and scarcity. This event showed his strategic acumen and his understanding of the economic interdependencies of the colonial powers.

The Capture of *La Concorde*

Another notorious episode was Blackbeard's capture of the French slave ship *La Concorde*, which he would transform into the infamous *Queen Anne's Revenge*. This capture, likely occurring in the waters near Hispaniola, was a testament to his prowess and opportunism. He outfitted the ship with forty guns, making it one of the most formidable pirate ships in the Caribbean.

The End of Blackbeard

Blackbeard's reign of terror came to an end in 1718. Following a fierce battle near Ocracoke Island in North Carolina, where Lieutenant Robert Maynard of the Royal Navy confronted him, Blackbeard was killed. His death was as dramatic as his life—it is said that he sustained multiple gunshots and sword wounds before finally succumbing. With his death, an era of piracy symbolically came to an end.

Legacy and Impact on Hispaniola

Blackbeard's legacy in the Caribbean and around Hispaniola is enduring. He is remembered not just for his terrifying persona and bold actions but as a symbol of the lawlessness and rebellious spirit of the age of piracy. For Hispaniola, his presence and activities were part of the larger narrative of piracy that shaped the island's colonial history, influencing the Spanish Empire's defensive strategies and the island's role in the geopolitical dynamics of the Caribbean.

The tales of Blackbeard's exploits, including his interactions with Hispaniola, have become an integral part of the lore of the Golden Age of Piracy, capturing the imagination of generations and highlighting the complex interplay of power, rebellion, and adventure that defined this tumultuous era in maritime history.

Jean Lafitte: The Buccaneer of the Gulf

Jean Lafitte, often remembered as the Buccaneer of the Gulf, was a figure shrouded in mystery and intrigue. While his exploits were centered on the Gulf of Mexico, he was born in Hispaniola and knew the waters well.

His operations and influence reached into the Caribbean. He and his fleet often ventured near Hispaniola, preying on Spanish ships and disrupting trade routes. Lafitte's knowledge of the Gulf and Caribbean waters made him a formidable figure, adept at eluding naval patrols and capitalizing on the lucrative opportunities these waters offered.

The Barataria Bay and Smuggling Networks

Lafitte established a base in Barataria Bay, Louisiana, which became a hub for smuggling operations. These operations included goods and slaves that were often brought through Caribbean routes, including those near Hispaniola. His smuggling network was sophisticated, involving local and international contacts, and played a significant role in the economy of the region.

The Battle of New Orleans

Jean Lafitte's most famous moment came during the War of 1812, particularly at the Battle of New Orleans in 1815. In a surprising turn of events, Lafitte allied himself and his men with General Andrew Jackson's forces, fighting against the British. His participation was a strategic decision, offering him legitimacy and favor in the eyes of the United States government. This alliance showcased Lafitte's ability to navigate complex political landscapes and align himself with powerful allies when it suited his interests.

Eluding Capture and Legendary Status

Throughout his career, Lafitte remained an elusive figure, skillfully avoiding capture by both the American and British navies. His ability to operate on the fringes of legality, coupled with his bold actions, contributed to his legendary status. He became a symbol of the romanticized pirate, a hero to some and a villain to others.

Anne Bonny and Mary Read: The Female Pirates

Anne Bonny and Mary Read stand out in the predominantly male world of piracy for their bravery, skill, and defiance of the social norms of their time. Their stories are not just tales of piracy but narratives of women challenging the boundaries of their societal roles.

Anne Bonny, born in Ireland and raised in the Carolinas, broke away from a conventional life to join the pirate world. Known for her fiery temper and formidable personality, she became involved with the pirate John "Calico Jack" Rackham and soon joined his crew.

Mary Read's journey to piracy was different. Disguised as a man for most of her life, she found herself in the British military before turning to piracy. Like Bonny, she joined Calico Jack's crew. Her true gender was discovered, but her place among the pirates was firmly established due to her fighting prowess.

Bonny and Read were integral members of Calico Jack's crew, participating in numerous raids and battles in the Caribbean. Their presence on the ship was initially a closely guarded secret but eventually became known. Their reputations for courage and combat skills were formidable, making them respected and feared figures among fellow pirates and targets.

The Capture and Trial

The end of Bonny and Read's piratical exploits came with the capture of Calico Jack's ship in 1720. During the capture, it was reported that Bonny and Read were among the few who actively fought against the naval forces, while many of their male counterparts were too intoxicated to fight.

Their trial was a sensational event, drawing considerable attention. Both women were found guilty but escaped execution by revealing that they were pregnant. Their ultimate fates remain a subject of speculation and legend, adding to their mystique.

Legacy and Impact

While Anne Bonny and Mary Read's direct impact on Hispaniola is less documented, their stories contribute significantly to the broader narrative of piracy in the Caribbean. They challenged the gender norms of their time, showing that women could be just as bold and fearsome as their male counterparts in the world of piracy.

Their legacy endures in the form of numerous books, films, and folklore, where they are often depicted as emblematic of female rebellion and resilience. The tales of Anne Bonny and Mary Read continue to captivate and inspire, serving as reminders of the diverse and often unexpected characters who played roles in the history of the Caribbean and piracy.

The Impact of These Pirates

The legends and tales of these pirates added to the folklore of the Caribbean. Stories of buried treasures and swashbuckling adventures captured the imagination of both locals and people far beyond the island, contributing to the mystique of the Caribbean as a region filled with danger and adventure.

As the Golden Age of piracy came to a close, largely due to increased naval patrols and crackdowns by colonial powers, the legacy of these pirates lingered in Hispaniola's history. They left behind tales of daring exploits, impacting the cultural heritage of the island and shaping perceptions of this era in Caribbean history.

Smuggling as Resistance to Spanish Rule

During the colonial era, the Caribbean witnessed a flourishing underground world of smuggling, significantly challenging Spanish rule, particularly in Hispaniola. This illicit trade had profound implications for the island's economy and society.

Spain, aiming to control and profit from its New World colonies, had established a stringent trade monopoly. The Casa de Contratación, or House of Trade, regulated all commerce between Spain and its colonies. This system dictated what goods could be traded, set prices, and levied high taxes. However, these restrictions were not well-received by the colonists in Hispaniola. They found the policies limiting, as they caused shortages of essential goods and inflated prices due to the monopoly.

Smuggling as a Response to Trade Limitations

In response to these constraints, smuggling became a widespread practice among Hispaniola's colonists. Denied the freedom to trade openly with other European nations, they began to clandestinely trade with British, French, and Dutch merchants. This smuggling involved secretly importing goods that were either too costly or unavailable through Spanish channels and exporting local commodities like sugar and tobacco.

Smuggling operations in Hispaniola were sophisticated and covert. Smugglers used the island's intricate coastline, with its numerous hidden coves and secluded beaches, to their advantage. They developed a network of secret routes and safe harbors for receiving smuggled goods. These operations required a high level of coordination and often relied on the complicity of local officials, some of whom were willing to ignore smuggling in exchange for bribes or a share in the profits.

The rise of smuggling in Hispaniola had a significant economic impact. It provided the colonists with access to a wider range of goods at more affordable prices, thereby improving their quality of life. However, for the Spanish authorities, smuggling posed a substantial problem. It eroded the effectiveness of the Casa de Contratación and led to the loss of considerable revenue from customs duties, which were crucial to the Spanish Crown's finances. The inability of the Spanish to control these illicit activities weakened their economic grip on the colony and undermined their authority. The illicit trade also diverted wealth to Spain's European rivals, who were more than willing to trade with the colonists in Hispaniola, defying Spanish regulations.

Expansion of Smuggling Networks

Smuggling in Hispaniola evolved into an extensive network encompassing not only local colonists but also international traders. These networks became increasingly sophisticated, involving a wide array of participants from different backgrounds, including European merchants, local traders, and even some colonial officials. The involvement of officials, often covertly supporting or turning a blind eye to smuggling, further undermined the legitimacy of the Spanish colonial administration.

Cultural and Social Impact

Smuggling brought about a cultural and social shift in Hispaniola. It introduced a variety of foreign goods and influences, contributing to the cultural diversity of the island. The act of smuggling also fostered a spirit of independence among the colonists, gradually eroding their loyalty to the Spanish Crown. This burgeoning independent streak was a precursor to broader sentiments of autonomy and self-governance.

The limitations imposed by Spanish trade policies, coupled with the benefits reaped from smuggling, contributed to growing discontent among the colonists. This dissatisfaction was not limited to economic grievances; it encompassed a desire for greater political and social freedoms. The success of smuggling operations demonstrated the colonists' capability to manage their affairs and challenged the Spanish Crown's absolute control over its colonies.

The widespread smuggling in Hispaniola played a role in shifting the power dynamics in the Caribbean. It exposed the vulnerabilities of Spanish colonial rule and highlighted the limitations of its mercantilist policies. Other European powers, recognizing the weakening Spanish hold, began to assert their influence more aggressively in the region, leading to increased competition and conflict.

Legacy of Smuggling in Hispaniola

The era of smuggling in Hispaniola marked a significant chapter in the island's history, weakening Spanish colonial control and contributing to the reshaping of the Caribbean's economic and political landscape. This period of clandestine trade and growing colonial discontent set the stage for the subsequent contest between European powers for control of the island, a contest that would further define the region's history.

The Struggle for Hispaniola – Early European Rivalries

Hispaniola, with its strategic position in the heart of the Caribbean, became a focal point for European powers in the colonial era. The island's rich resources and significant location turned it into a battleground for control among Spain, France, England, and the Netherlands.

Spanish Dominance and Early Challenges

Initially, Hispaniola was predominantly under Spanish control. The Spanish established their first New World colony in Santo Domingo, on the eastern part of the island. However, the lure of Hispaniola's resources, including its fertile lands ideal for sugar cultivation and strategic maritime location, did not escape the attention of other European powers.

French Encroachment and Settlements

The French were the first to challenge Spanish dominance effectively. They began by establishing unofficial settlements on the less guarded western part of the island. These settlements gradually grew, siphoning off wealth that could have gone to the Spanish Crown. The French presence on Hispaniola was initially ignored or tolerated by Spain, partly due to the challenges Spain faced in maintaining control over its vast empire.

Economic and Strategic Significance

Hispaniola's economic significance stemmed from its potential to develop into a booming sugar colony, similar to other Caribbean islands like Barbados and Jamaica. Moreover, its location made it a key strategic point for controlling the passage through the Caribbean Sea, a route crucial for transatlantic trade.

The English, recognizing Hispaniola's importance, also sought to establish a presence on the island. Their attempts led to confrontations with the Spanish forces, turning the waters around Hispaniola into scenes of naval skirmishes and battles. Although the English were unable to secure a permanent foothold on Hispaniola, their persistent efforts weakened Spanish control and opened opportunities for other powers.

The Dutch, major players in global trade, were more interested in the economic opportunities Hispaniola offered than territorial control. They became key suppliers of arms and goods to other European powers and local colonists, often circumventing Spanish restrictions. Their involvement further complicated the power dynamics on the island, making Hispaniola a nexus of not just colonial ambition but extensive smuggling networks.

The Local Impact of Rivalries

The ongoing European rivalries had significant impacts on Hispaniola's local population. Colonial ambitions led to militarization and fortification of the island, diverting resources from other developmental needs. The presence of multiple European powers also influenced the cultural and social landscape, introducing diverse influences that would shape Hispaniola's identity.

During this period, Hispaniola was not merely a passive backdrop to European rivalries; it was an active and contested space where the future of the Caribbean was being shaped. The struggle for control over Hispaniola laid the foundation for future conflicts and negotiations, significantly influencing the island's trajectory in the colonial era. The next segment will further explore how these early rivalries evolved into a formal division of the island and the lasting effects of this contest on Hispaniola's development and path toward the modern era.

The Division of Hispaniola and the Shaping of a New Caribbean Order

As European rivalries intensified over Hispaniola, the struggle for control eventually led to a formal division of the island, reshaping its destiny and contributing to the emergence of a new order in the Caribbean.

The ongoing contest for Hispaniola reached a pivotal point with the Treaty of Ryswick in 1697, which officially recognized French control over the western third of the island, renamed Saint-Domingue. This division was a significant moment in Caribbean history, as it ended the Spanish monopoly over Hispaniola and acknowledged the presence of another colonial power. The Spanish retained control of the eastern part, Santo Domingo, but the balance of power on the island had shifted. By 1795, the French earned control of two-thirds of the island.

Saint-Domingue's Rise and Santo Domingo's Decline

The French colony of Saint-Domingue rapidly grew to become one of the richest colonies in the Caribbean, outshining its Spanish counterpart in wealth and production. Fueled by the booming sugar industry and extensive use of enslaved African labor, Saint-Domingue became a cornerstone of the French colonial empire. In contrast, the Spanish side of the island, Santo Domingo, experienced relative economic stagnation, as Spain's focus shifted to its mainland and other territories.

Impact on Colonial Dynamics and Trade

The division of Hispaniola into French and Spanish territories altered colonial dynamics in the region. It intensified competition among European powers, as they sought to protect and expand their respective interests in the Caribbean. Trade routes, alliances, and economic policies were all affected by the presence of two colonial powers on a single island.

The division also had profound cultural and social ramifications. Saint-Domingue developed a distinct Franco-Caribbean culture, influenced by African traditions brought by enslaved peoples, French colonial practices, and the realities of plantation life. Meanwhile, the

Spanish side maintained a more traditional Spanish colonial culture. These differing cultural identities contributed to a diverse and complex social fabric on Hispaniola.

The Path to Revolution and Independence

The contrasting fortunes of the French and Spanish sides of Hispaniola set the stage for future upheavals. Saint-Domingue, with its harsh plantation system and significant population of enslaved Africans, became a hotbed for revolutionary ideas. These simmering tensions eventually led to the Haitian Revolution in the late eighteenth century, a landmark event that would change the fate of Hispaniola and send shockwaves across the colonial world.

Legacy of the Division

The division of Hispaniola and the ensuing developments had lasting impacts on the Caribbean. They underscored the fragility of colonial systems based on exploitation and the potential for revolutionary change. Hispaniola's split into two distinct entities, each with its own trajectory, became a symbol of the broader struggles and transformations occurring throughout the Caribbean.

The contest for Hispaniola and its eventual division marked the end of an era and the beginning of a new chapter in Caribbean history. It highlighted the complexities of colonial rule, the impact of international rivalries, and the beginnings of the region's journey toward self-determination and independence.

Chapter 6 – Struggle for Sovereignty

The Dominican Republic's history unfolds like a rich and complex story, full of resilience, change, and a relentless drive for identity and self-determination. Born from the shadows of colonial dominance and dramatically influenced by the monumental changes in neighboring nations, the Dominican Republic has been on an extraordinary journey. This chapter explores the pivotal moments that have defined this nation—from the profound reverberations of the Haitian Revolution to the passionate pursuit of independence and the formative years of nation-building that followed.

In the nineteenth and early twentieth centuries, the Dominican Republic navigated a challenging course. It's a story of a people united in their effort to forge a nation, wrestling with the trials of newfound independence and the desire to shape a unified national identity. Their path was marked by courageous leaders, a reawakening of cultural identity, and an unyielding drive toward sovereignty.

As we unfold the pages of Dominican history, we see not just the hurdles and conflicts encountered but the remarkable tenacity and spirit of the Dominican people. Their journey is a powerful testament to their resilience against obstacles and their unwavering dedication to building a nation true to its unique past while boldly stepping into the future.

The Haitian Revolution and Its Impact on Hispaniola

The Haitian Revolution had far-reaching effects on Hispaniola, igniting a series of changes that altered the trajectory of their future. This part of the story delves into the origins, intense struggles, and far-reaching impacts of this revolution on Hispaniola's social, political, and cultural landscapes.

The Course of the Revolution

In 1791, the seeds of a monumental upheaval were sown in the fertile grounds of Saint-Domingue (the eastern French side). Here, amidst the lush plantations that belied a cruel reality, the Haitian Revolution burst forth—a vibrant yet tumultuous canvas of human struggle and aspiration.

The revolution was kindled by the unbearable harshness of slavery and inspired by the ideals of liberty and equality emanating from the French Revolution. In Saint-Domingue, most of the population—enslaved Africans and those of African descent—stood on the precipice of a historic uprising. They were set to challenge not just the inhumanity of the plantation system but the very foundations of colonial authority.

What ensued was a complex, visceral conflict that spanned over a decade, painting the island with the struggles and hopes of its people. The rebellion saw fierce confrontations between the enslaved, free people of color, and colonial forces. This era was also marked by the intervention of international powers like Spain, Britain, and France, each drawn by their interests and agendas.

Emerging from this crucible of conflict were towering figures such as Toussaint L'Ouverture, Jean-Jacques Dessalines, and Henri Christophe. These leaders became emblematic of the indomitable will for freedom, guiding a revolution that was as much a fight for rights as a reclamation of human dignity.

The Abolition of Slavery and the Birth of a Nation

One of the revolution's most profound achievements was the abolition of slavery in Saint-Domingue. This act resonated far beyond the colony's borders, challenging slaveholding societies across the Americas and Europe and reshaping the discourse on human rights and liberty. The struggle and sacrifices in the French colony culminated in 1804 with a declaration that resonated through the annals of history—the birth of Haiti, the world's first Black republic and a beacon of hope for oppressed peoples everywhere.

The Revolutionaries

Toussaint L'Ouverture

Born into slavery in Saint-Domingue in the early 1740s, L'Ouverture experienced the brutal realities of plantation life. However, his enslavement did not quell his thirst for knowledge and desire for freedom. He educated himself, a rarity among enslaved people, and this education laid the foundation for his future role as a revolutionary leader.

L'Ouverture emerged as a leader in the Haitian Revolution in 1791. Initially, he worked as a medic for the rebel forces, but his natural leadership skills and military acumen soon propelled him to the forefront of the uprising. He was a master strategist, known for his diplomatic skills and ability to navigate the complex political landscape of colonial Saint-Domingue.

Under L'Ouverture's leadership, the revolutionaries fought against various colonial powers, including the French, Spanish, and British. He was instrumental in crafting alliances, orchestrating military campaigns, and working toward the goal of an independent Haiti. L'Ouverture's vision extended beyond mere military victory; he sought to build a society based on equality and justice.

L'Ouverture eventually became the governor-general of Saint-Domingue, bringing significant reforms to the island. He worked to restore the economy, rebuild infrastructure, and promote policies that aimed at social and racial equality. His administration, though autocratic, was marked by efforts to improve the lives of the formerly enslaved and create a self-sustaining nation.

In a twist of fate, L'Ouverture was captured by the French in 1802 and deported to France, where he died in prison in 1803. His death, however, did not halt the revolution. It continued under new leaders and ultimately led to the declaration of Haitian independence in 1804.

Toussaint L'Ouverture's legacy transcends his role in the Haitian Revolution. He is remembered as a symbol of the fight against oppression, a visionary leader who challenged the prevailing norms of his time, and a foundational figure in the quest for Black freedom and sovereignty. His life and achievements continue to inspire movements for justice and equality around the world, embodying the enduring spirit of resistance against tyranny and injustice.

Jean-Jacques Dessalines

Dessalines was born into slavery in Saint-Domingue and lived under the oppressive conditions of the French colonial system. He joined the Haitian Revolution early in its course, initially serving under leaders like Toussaint L'Ouverture. Dessalines was known for his fierce fighting spirit and his unwavering dedication to the cause of freedom for the enslaved.

After the capture of L'Ouverture in 1802, Dessalines emerged as the primary leader of the revolution. He was a formidable military commander, known for his ruthless tactics and strategic acumen. Under his leadership, the revolutionaries intensified their campaign against the French colonial forces, leading to significant victories that were crucial in the fight for independence.

Dessalines declared the independence of Haiti on January 1, 1804, marking the end of French colonial rule and the establishment of the first free Black republic in the world. This historic moment was a powerful symbol of the triumph of the enslaved over their oppressors and a monumental achievement in the history of the Atlantic world.

As the leader of independent Haiti, Dessalines assumed the title of Emperor Jacques I. His rule was characterized by efforts to strengthen the new nation, though his administration faced numerous challenges, including internal divisions and the threat of foreign intervention. Dessalines' reign was short-lived; he was assassinated in 1806. However, his legacy endures as a key architect of Haitian independence and a symbol of resistance against colonialism and slavery.

Henri Christophe

Christophe was born into slavery on the island of Grenada but found his way to Saint-Domingue, where he became deeply involved in the revolutionary struggle. His military prowess and leadership skills quickly became apparent, and he rose through the ranks to become a key commander in the revolutionary forces, fighting alongside leaders like Toussaint L'Ouverture and Jean-Jacques Dessalines.

During the Haitian Revolution, Christophe distinguished himself as a formidable military leader. His contributions were crucial in several significant battles against the French colonial forces. Christophe's leadership was instrumental in achieving the victories that ultimately led to Haiti's independence.

Following Haiti's independence in 1804 and the subsequent assassination of Dessalines in 1806, the country faced internal divisions. Christophe emerged as the leader of Northern Haiti, establishing his capital at Cap-Haïtien. In 1811, he declared himself King Henri I and set about building the Kingdom of Haiti, with a focus on strengthening and modernizing the state.

As king, Christophe implemented various economic reforms to revitalize Haiti's economy, which included improving agriculture and infrastructure. He is particularly renowned for constructing the Citadelle Laferrière, a massive fortress in northern Haiti, and the Sans-Souci Palace, both of which stand today as symbols of Haiti's post-independence resilience and Christophe's ambition.

Henri Christophe's rule was marked by efforts to establish a strong, stable government and to promote education and the arts. However, his reign was also characterized by authoritarianism, and he faced opposition from those who resisted his rigid control. In 1820, facing a debilitating illness and the prospect of a coup, Christophe tragically took his own life.

Christophe's legacy in Haitian history is complex. He is remembered both for his contributions to Haiti's fight for independence and his ambitious, though sometimes harsh, efforts to build a nation from the ruins of colonialism. His life and leadership reflect the challenges faced by Haiti in its early years as the world's first Black republic, navigating the delicate balance between autocracy and nation-building.

Ripples Across Hispaniola: Impact on Spanish Santo Domingo

The eastern half of Hispaniola, Spanish Santo Domingo (former Spanish colony), was not untouched by the reverberations of this upheaval. The triumph of the Haitian Revolution in Saint Domingue paved the way for new social and political ideas by challenging the entrenched systems of racial hierarchy and colonialism. It inspired a sense of pride and a quest for self-determination among the populations in both parts of the island. Among the enslaved and free people of color, the revolution was a beacon of hope and a powerful example of what could be achieved. It sparked discussions about freedom, equality, and human rights, planting the early seeds of an independence movement.

Conversely, it sowed seeds of fear and apprehension among the Spanish rulers and white settlers. The Spanish colonial authorities, witnessing the upheaval and its outcomes, intensified their efforts to maintain order and prevent a similar uprising. This led to stricter governance and an increased military presence. The white and Creole populations, apprehensive about the possibility of rebellion, also supported measures to strengthen defenses and safeguard their properties and way of life.

The revolution also transformed the economic landscape of Hispaniola. The destruction of plantations and the shift in the labor system in Saint-Domingue disrupted traditional trade patterns. This shift provided an impetus for economic changes in Santo Domingo, which began to move away from a strict plantation-based economy.

The Spanish administration in Santo Domingo, in response to the changing times, began to reassess its colonial strategies. There was a recognition that the old ways of rigid control might no longer be sustainable. Efforts were made to placate the local population and prevent discontent from turning into rebellion. These efforts included limited reforms and attempts to boost the local economy, although they were often hindered by ingrained colonial attitudes and interests.

The relationship between Haiti and Spanish Santo Domingo during this era was complex. It was marked by moments of tension and discord, especially over border disputes and clashing ideologies. Yet, interwoven with these conflicts were threads of cooperation and mutual support. Both sides of Hispaniola were navigating a challenging dance of diplomacy and shared struggles, balancing their internal aspirations and agendas with the pressures of external colonial forces.

The Spark of Dominican Independence

Wider geopolitical shifts, such as the Napoleonic Wars, rattled the foundations of colonial empires. Spain's grip on its colonies weakened, leading to a period of political uncertainty and creating a window of opportunity for change. The restoration of the Spanish monarchy, attempting to reassert its authority, further stirred the pot of political discontent in Spanish Santo Domingo (the former Spanish colony of the island). These global events, playing out across oceans, had ripple effects that reached the shores of Hispaniola, igniting a spark of resistance and hope among its people.

Key Figures in the Early Independence Movement

In the Dominican fight for independence, several remarkable individuals stand out, each bringing their unique passion, vision, and resolve to the forefront. These were not just leaders; they were the heart and soul of the movement, their lives intertwining with the destiny of a nation yearning to be free.

Juan Pablo Duarte: At the heart of this struggle was Juan Pablo Duarte, often hailed as the father of Dominican independence. Born into affluence, Duarte's education abroad exposed him to the revolutionary winds of Enlightenment thought. Embracing ideals of liberty, equality, and brotherhood, he returned to Santo Domingo not just as a son of privilege but as a fervent advocate for freedom. His drive and dedication led to the creation of La Trinitaria, a clandestine group committed to severing the chains of Haitian rule and birthing a free Dominican Republic.

Ramón Matías Mella: Alongside Duarte stood Ramón Matías Mella, a man whose patriotism was matched only by his strategic brilliance. Mella, a fervent nationalist, was the sinew and muscle in the resistance against Haitian occupation and, later, the Spanish resurgence. His name became synonymous with unwavering commitment to the Dominican cause, etched forever in the annals of history for his role in pivotal battles and the proclamation of independence in 1844.

Francisco del Rosario Sánchez: Francisco del Rosario Sánchez, a lawyer with the gift of oratory, emerged as another pillar of the movement. As a key member of La Trinitaria and a trusted ally of Duarte, Sánchez's eloquence and legal acumen were instrumental in galvanizing support for the cause. His leadership shone brightest when Duarte was forced into exile, and his contribution to drafting a declaration of independence was a testament to his passion for a sovereign Dominican Republic.

María Trinidad Sánchez: Behind these men was a woman of quiet strength and courage —María Trinidad Sánchez. As Francisco del Rosario Sánchez's aunt, she played a crucial but often overlooked role in the independence movement. Her support of La Trinitaria's activities, often at great personal risk, symbolizes the vital but unrecognized efforts of women in the quest for Dominican independence.

Pedro Santana: The early stages of the independence movement also saw the rise of Pedro Santana, a military figure whose legacy is mired in controversy. Initially a supporter of the anti-Haitian cause, his later actions, including the re-invitation of Spanish rule, cast a shadow over his contributions. Yet, his early military successes were undeniably pivotal in shaping the Dominican Republic's path to independence.

These figures, each with their own stories, dreams, and struggles, were the architects of a new Dominican Republic. Their diverse backgrounds wove together a movement that stood resilient against colonial oppression. They were more than just architects of independence; they were the embodiment of a nation's aspiration for freedom and the right to determine its destiny.

Early Movements and Conspiracies

This period saw the formation of several movements and conspiracies aimed at achieving independence. These efforts were initially small and localized, involving clandestine meetings and the spread of revolutionary ideas. While many of these early attempts were suppressed by colonial authorities, they laid the foundation for more organized and widespread resistance.

Parallel to the political movements, there was a cultural and intellectual awakening in Spanish Santo Domingo. Literature, arts, and the press began to reflect and foster a sense of Dominican identity, separate from colonial influences. This cultural shift was instrumental in building a national consciousness that would underpin the fight for independence.

The early stages of the fight for Dominican independence were marked by three things: nationalist sentiments, intellectual discourse, and political activism. These elements combined to form the basis of a movement that would grow in strength and determination. This led to more organized and decisive actions in the quest for a free and independent Dominican Republic.

Escalation of the Independence Movement in the Dominican Republic

As the fight for Dominican independence intensified, the movement transitioned from the realm of intellectual debate and clandestine planning to overt political and military action. This segment explores the escalation of the movement, highlighting the significant events and challenges that propelled the Dominican Republic toward its eventual independence.

La Trinitaria, founded by Juan Pablo Duarte, played a pivotal role in escalating the independence movement, operating through a network of cells to evade detection. Its members, drawn from various segments of society, worked tirelessly to spread the message of independence, galvanize public support, and plan for armed insurrection.

The independence movement took a more public and assertive turn as members of La Trinitaria began openly advocating for the cause. The increasing boldness of the independence activists led to heightened tensions with the Haitian authorities, resulting in crackdowns, arrests, and the exile of several key leaders, including Duarte. Despite these setbacks, the movement continued to gain traction among the populace.

The Haitian occupation, while initially limiting the prospects for a successful rebellion, inadvertently helped solidify support for the independence movement. Policies imposed by the Haitian government, including heavy taxation and attempts at cultural assimilation, were deeply unpopular and fueled resentment among the Dominican populace. This growing discontent provided fertile ground for the seeds of rebellion sown by La Trinitaria.

The fight for independence was fraught with challenges. The nascent Dominican forces had to contend with not only the Haitian army but also internal divisions and the complexities of international diplomacy. The involvement of foreign powers, each with its interests in the Caribbean, added another layer of complexity to the struggle.

Toward the Declaration of Independence

Despite the obstacles, the resolve of the Dominican rebels remained unshaken. Key victories and strategic leadership gradually turned the tide in their favor.

The conflict began with a series of strategic uprisings orchestrated by Dominican rebels. These uprisings were carefully planned to maximize impact and rally support from various parts of the country. The rebels, although initially outnumbered and facing a well-established military force, demonstrated remarkable resilience and tactical ingenuity.

Several key battles during this period were instrumental in shaping the course of the war. Leaders like Francisco del Rosario Sánchez and Ramón Matías Mella emerged as strategic military minds, leading successful assaults against Haitian forces. Their victories in battles like the one at Cabeza de Las Marías galvanized the rebel forces and boosted morale.

The decisive moment came with the taking of the Ozama Fortress in Santo Domingo on February 27, 1844. This victory was crucial and symbolized the fall of Haitian authority in the colony. That same night, the rebels, amidst celebratory gunfire and jubilation, proclaimed the independence of the Dominican Republic.

The declaration on February 27, 1844, marked the birth of the Dominican Republic as a sovereign nation. It was a momentous event, reflecting the aspirations of a people long yearning for self-determination. The declaration not only signified political autonomy but also the rebirth of Dominican culture and identity.

Consolidating Dominican Independence

Following its declaration of independence in 1844, the Dominican Republic faced the complex task of consolidating its newfound sovereignty. This segment examines the challenges and milestones during this crucial period in shaping the nation's future.

In the immediate aftermath of independence, the Dominican Republic's first government was established. Leaders of the independence movement had to quickly transition from rebellion to state-building. This involved forming governmental institutions, creating a legal framework, and establishing mechanisms for international diplomacy.

Despite the declaration of independence, the threat from Haiti persisted. Haitian forces, unwilling to accept the loss of the eastern part of Hispaniola, launched several invasions to regain control. These invasions forced the nascent Dominican government to focus heavily on defense and military organization, a challenge that tested the resilience and resourcefulness of the young republic.

The new Dominican Republic also faced internal challenges, including political infighting and regional rivalries. Different factions, each with its vision for the country, vied for power and influence.

As the Dominican Republic carved out its place in the world, the quest for international recognition took center stage. It was a dance of diplomacy, as the young nation reached out to establish its voice among the global community. Building relationships with countries like the United States and across Europe wasn't just about politics; it was about standing proud as a new, sovereign nation on the world stage.

Founding the Early Republic Era of the Dominican Republic

The early years of the Dominican Republic were consumed with laying the foundations for a stable and functional state. This involved establishing new political institutions, drafting a constitution, and creating a legal system that would govern the newly independent nation. The first Dominican Constitution, adopted in 1844, was a significant milestone, reflecting the republic's aspirations and values.

The new republic faced the daunting task of rebuilding and diversifying its economy. The area had been heavily reliant on agriculture, particularly sugar and tobacco. Efforts were made to revive agriculture, particularly the cultivation of cash crops like tobacco and sugar. Efforts were also made to stimulate trade, attract foreign investment, and develop infrastructure to support economic growth. However, these efforts were often hindered by political instability and limited resources.

Leadership struggles and frequent changes in government marked this period. Figures like Pedro Santana and Buenaventura Báez emerged as dominant leaders, each with their own approach to governance and vision for the country. Their leadership was marked by periods of progress but also by controversial decisions, including Santana's annexation of the republic to Spain in 1861 (more on that in the next chapter).

The Dominican Republic's struggle to maintain sovereignty and establish a national identity was central to the early republic era. The threat of re-colonization or foreign intervention was a constant concern, influencing foreign policy and national defense strategies. The quest to forge a distinct Dominican identity, separate from both Haitian and Spanish influences, was reflected in cultural policies, education, and public discourse.

Social Changes and Cultural Evolution

With independence, the Dominican Republic began a vibrant journey of social and cultural reawakening. Emancipation from Haitian rule and the end of Spanish colonialism prompted a reevaluation of social structures and racial dynamics. Cultural evolution, influenced by the independence movement and the diverse history of the island, began to solidify a unique Dominican culture, encompassing music, literature, and the arts. Schools became the nurseries of the nation's future, the arts flourished as expressions of newfound freedom, and public works bonded communities, knitting together a diverse and dynamic society.

Chapter 7 – Political Insecurity and the Quest for Stability

In the nineteenth and early twentieth centuries, the Dominican Republic's story unfolds like a dramatic saga, rich with transformation and resilience. This era, a defining chapter in the nation's history, showcases the unyielding spirit of a people and a land navigating the turbulent seas of change. It's a story that weaves through the aftermath of independence, with its blend of chaos and hope, to the formidable task of nation-building.

Imagine a nation, fresh from the chains of colonial rule, striving to find its footing. The Dominican Republic, in these years, was a canvas of human endeavor—each brushstroke representing the efforts of those who dared to dream of a stable, flourishing future. This period was more than a sequence of events; it was the shaping of a nation's soul.

The journey was far from smooth. The Dominican Republic faced its share of trials—the internal tumult of political rivalries, the heavy hand of external influences, and the daunting task of crafting an identity from a fragmented past. Yet, in every challenge, the Dominican character shone through, resilient and hopeful.

This wasn't just a political journey; it was a cultural renaissance, an economic awakening. From the vibrant streets of Santo Domingo to the rural heartlands, a sense of Dominican identity began to take root and flourish. Arts, music, and literature blossomed, painting a picture of a nation rich in culture and proud of its heritage.

And so, the Dominican Republic, through these transformative years, wasn't merely surviving; it was sculpting its place in the world. Each decision, each struggle, was a step toward carving out a modern state— one that balanced the dreams of its people with the realities of a complex global stage.

This chapter in the Dominican Republic's history highlights the nation's unwavering commitment to sovereignty and self-determination, painting a vivid picture of a country striving to realize its potential while honoring its rich heritage. The narrative of these crucial years provides profound insights into the building blocks of the nation's present and future.

The Nineteenth Century's Revolving Door of Rulers and Occupations

The nineteenth century in the Dominican Republic was characterized by a period of significant political instability, marked by a revolving door of rulers and occupations. This segment explores the tumultuous political landscape of the Dominican Republic during this era, highlighting the key factors contributing to this instability.

Following its declaration of independence in 1844, the Dominican Republic struggled to establish a stable and effective government. Leadership changed hands frequently, often through coups, insurrections, and foreign interventions, rather than democratic processes. This constant change in leadership hindered the development of strong political institutions and the policies necessary for national stability.

The political scene in the Dominican Republic during this time was dominated by caudillos (strongmen) who wielded significant power. These leaders often ruled through personalist regimes, placing their interests above national welfare. Their governance style contributed to a cycle of political and economic instability, as each leader's rise to power often came at the cost of civil unrest and disruption.

Foreign powers, notably Spain, the United States, and Haiti, took advantage of the Dominican Republic's instability. These nations, seeking to expand their influence in the Caribbean, intervened in Dominican affairs, further complicating the political situation.

Economic Challenges and Political Strife

Economic difficulties, including debt crises and reliance on volatile export markets, exacerbated the Dominican Republic's political instability. Leaders like Buenaventura Báez attempted to address these economic problems through foreign loans and treaties, often leading to increased foreign influence and internal dissent. The interplay between economic hardship and political maneuvering created an environment where short-term gains were often prioritized over long-term national stability.

The frequent changes in rulers and political direction had a profound impact on Dominican society. It hindered the development of consistent governance policies, leaving many national issues, such as education, infrastructure, and public services, unaddressed. The populace, facing the consequences of political instability, grew increasingly disillusioned with its leadership, fostering a climate of mistrust and skepticism toward the government.

The nineteenth century's revolving door of rulers and occupations in the Dominican Republic set the stage for a century fraught with political upheaval. It was a time when the foundations of the nation were tested, and the quest for a stable and effective governance system became a paramount concern. This period laid the groundwork for the subsequent chapters in Dominican history, which would include continued struggles but also efforts toward establishing a more stable and prosperous state.

Continued Struggles for Power and Stability in the Late Nineteenth Century

As the Dominican Republic progressed through the latter half of the nineteenth century, the nation continued grappling with political instability and the challenges of establishing stable governance.

The pattern of frequent leadership changes persisted. In the bustling heart of the Dominican Republic, the halls of power were witness to a whirlwind of change. Here, a parade of leaders and councils rose and fell, each grappling with the reins of a nation in flux. It was a time when the presidential chair was seldom warm before the next change, a vivid illustration of the tumultuous political landscape.

Picture a country where governments flickered like candles in the wind—brief, bright, and often extinguished by the gusts of internal strife. Political battles were waged not only in the corridors of power but in the streets, where the voices of the people echoed with demands for change. Coups and uprisings were as frequent as the Caribbean storms, sweeping leaders away in their fervor.

In this ever-shifting scene, each president or council endeavored to guide the Dominican Republic through a maze of challenges. Their tenures might have been short, but their impact lingered, weaving into the nation's complex tapestry. Economic puzzles and social quandaries awaited solutions, even as the political ground shifted ceaselessly underfoot.

This was more than just a sequence of governments; it was the pulse of a nation seeking stability and progress amidst the passionate tides of change.

The Dominican Republic's political instability was further exacerbated by deep-seated regional and factional rivalries. These regional divisions were not just political but also had cultural and economic dimensions, contributing to the difficulty of forming a unified national government.

The chess board laid over the lands of the Dominican Republic also had foreign players. In the nineteenth and early twentieth centuries, the nation was not only grappling with its own identity and challenges but also navigating the murky waters of foreign influence.

Imagine the island as a coveted jewel, its strategic location and economic potential catching the keen eyes of distant powers. European nations and the United States, driven by their own interests, reached out their hands to subtly tilt the scales of Dominican politics.

The air in the halls of governance was thick with diplomatic maneuvering as foreign envoys and local leaders danced a delicate waltz of diplomacy and interests. Money, as always, spoke a persuasive language, with financial aid and control becoming tools in the hands of those seeking to sway the direction of the young nation.

At times, this foreign involvement was more overt, casting long shadows of military vessels on Dominican shores. These instances were stark reminders of the complex interplay of local aspirations and global ambitions.

For the Dominican Republic, this period was more than a struggle for political stability; it was a continuous effort to carve out a space for autonomous decision-making, a place where the voice of the nation could ring out clear and strong, unclouded by the chorus of foreign interests.

Efforts Toward Constitutionalism and Reform

Against this backdrop of political unrest, a determined push for stability and reform was underway. The nation's leaders, aware of the need for solid foundations, embarked on a mission to craft the pillars of a stronger, more resilient government.

Picture a series of new constitutions, each born out of the fervent discussions and debates of those seeking a better future. With each constitution, the Dominican Republic took steps toward framing a system that upheld civil liberties and the rule of law—ideals that were eagerly sought amid turbulence.

Of course, the road to reform was far from smooth. Each attempt to establish a more robust governance structure encountered its share of hurdles. Challenges emerged not just from within the tumultuous political arena but also from the complexities of implementing these grand visions into practical reality.

Yet, despite these challenges, the efforts to draft and implement new constitutions signaled a significant shift. They reflected a collective aspiration to move beyond the instability of the past toward a future anchored in institutional strength and democratic principles.

Economic instability remained a significant challenge, influencing the political landscape. Issues like foreign debt, reliance on agricultural exports, and inadequate infrastructure continued to plague the country, often becoming focal points of political contention. The struggle to build a sustainable economy was closely intertwined with the quest for political stability.

The Dominican people, amidst these challenges, played a crucial role in the nation's political narrative. Popular movements, uprisings, and civic engagement were instrumental in shaping the political discourse, reflecting the populace's aspirations for stable and effective governance.

The Spanish Annexation of the Dominican Republic

The mid-nineteenth century in the Dominican Republic was a defining period marked by the controversial Spanish annexation, an event that significantly altered the nation's course. This segment explores the lead-up to annexation, the annexation itself, and its immediate repercussions.

The idea of annexation to Spain was driven partly by the internal strife and political instability in the Dominican Republic. Pedro Santana, a dominant figure in Dominican politics and a supporter of Spanish annexation, played a pivotal role in advocating for this move. He and his supporters believed that rejoining Spain would bring stability, protection, and economic benefits, helping to alleviate the chronic volatility that plagued the young nation.

In 1861, Santana officially initiated the process of returning the Dominican Republic to Spanish rule, a decision that was met with mixed reactions. While some segments of the population supported the annexation, hoping for stability and economic growth, others vehemently opposed it, viewing it as a betrayal of the hard-fought independence of 1844.

Spain's Re-establishment of Colonial Rule

The Spanish authorities worked swiftly to imprint their presence, re-establishing colonial systems and re-integrating the island into their empire. But this wasn't a mere administrative shuffle; it was a significant upheaval that touched every corner of Dominican society.

In towns and villages, the reassertion of Spanish rule was met with mixed reactions. For some, it brought hopes of stability and progress under a familiar colonial power. Yet for many others, it was a step backward, a move that threatened the hard-earned autonomy they had begun to cherish. This divide created ripples of tension across the country, as communities grappled with the realities of returning to a colonial regime.

Economically, the annexation's promise of prosperity and development rang hollow for many. The Dominican Republic's economy, largely dependent on a few cash crops, continued to face the same old problems. The Spanish policies did little to address these economic vulnerabilities, leaving many Dominicans to contend with the same challenges that had long hampered their economic growth.

The return to Spanish rule wasn't just a political maneuver; it was a moment that tested the resilience and aspirations of the Dominican people. It brought to the fore the contrasting visions of their future and set the stage for the continued struggle for self-determination and economic stability.

The Fight for Restoration and the War of Restoration

Resistance to Spanish rule began to mount almost immediately after the annexation. (The annexation came about in March, and the first rebellion broke out in May.) The resistance was fueled by a resurgence of nationalistic sentiment and the desire to reclaim the sovereignty that had been lost. This unrest laid the groundwork for the eventual fight to restore Dominican independence.

Opposition to Spanish rule steadily grew as the annexation failed to bring the promised stability and economic prosperity. The resistance was fueled by widespread dissatisfaction with the Spanish administration, economic exploitation, and the imposition of unfamiliar laws and customs. Key figures from the independence movement, including some who initially supported the annexation, began to organize and mobilize against Spanish rule.

A nationalist front began to form, uniting various factions that opposed the annexation. This front transcended previous political and regional divisions, bringing together a diverse coalition united by the common goal of restoring Dominican sovereignty. The movement was characterized by both peaceful advocacy and preparation for armed resistance.

The Grito de Capotillo and the Start of Armed Struggle

The struggle for independence reached a critical juncture with the Grito de Capotillo in 1863, a significant armed uprising against Spanish rule. This event marked the beginning of the Dominican War of Restoration. The insurgents were few and their resources limited, yet what they lacked in numbers and arms, they made up for with an unquenchable thirst for freedom and a steadfast belief in the right to self-govern.

On that fateful day of August 16, 1863, in the small town of Capotillo, these brave souls ignited a spark that would soon blaze across the nation. The uprising forever etched in history as the Grito de Capotillo was more than just a call to arms—it was a powerful declaration of a people's resolve to reclaim their sovereignty. The air rang with their cries for independence, a resounding "grito" that echoed the deepest desires of every Dominican heart.

Key figures in this uprising included Santiago Rodríguez, José Cabrera, Benito Monción, and Gregorio Luperón, among others. These leaders, along with a group of brave patriots, raised the Dominican flag at the Capotillo hill, signaling the start of an armed revolt. This act of defiance was a powerful symbol of resistance and the unyielding desire for national sovereignty.

The War of Restoration would last for two years. Dominicans from all walks of life joined the cause, fighting against Spanish forces in a bid to regain their independence. The war was characterized by guerrilla tactics, battles, and significant sacrifices made by the Dominican people.

The Grito de Capotillo is commemorated annually in the Dominican Republic as a national holiday. It is remembered not only as the start of the War of Restoration but also as a testament to the resilience and determination of the Dominican people in their quest for freedom and self-determination. The event stands as a pivotal moment in Dominican history, symbolizing the spirit of resistance and the enduring struggle for national identity and sovereignty.

Key Battles and Turning Points

The War of Restoration was marked by several significant battles and strategic victories that played pivotal roles in the Dominican Republic's struggle to regain independence. These encounters not only demonstrated the resilience and tactical ingenuity of the Dominican forces but also were crucial in shifting the momentum of the conflict.

Siege of Santiago

In September, a force of 6,000 Dominicans attacked the Fort San Luis in Santiago. Within ten days, the small garrison (800) and their reinforcements (2,000 soldiers) evacuated. With this success, the rebel forces established a new government the next day. Santana was denounced officially, although he had already been labeled as a traitor for leading the Spanish forces.

Naval Blockades and International Support

In addition to land battles, naval blockades and skirmishes played a significant role. Dominican forces, with limited naval capabilities, engaged in daring actions against Spanish ships, disrupting supply lines. The support of foreign nations, particularly Haiti, which provided sanctuary and support to Dominican forces, was instrumental in sustaining the restoration campaign.

The restoration movement also navigated complex international dynamics. Sympathy for the Dominican cause in other Caribbean nations and the United States played a role in the movement's favor. Diplomatic efforts were made to gain international support and recognition, which were crucial in legitimizing the fight for independence. With the end of the American Civil War, the Spanish government feared the US would join the conflict.

End of Spanish Rule and Restoration of Independence

After years of conflict, Spanish forces, facing mounting resistance and growing challenges in the Dominican Republic and abroad, finally capitulated. In March 1865, the Spanish government formally recognized the end of its rule over the Dominican Republic, leading to the restoration of Dominican independence.

The restoration of independence was a momentous achievement for the Dominican Republic. It reaffirmed the nation's sovereignty and marked the end of colonial rule. This period was crucial in shaping the Dominican Republic's national identity and set the stage for its future as an independent nation.

The Triumph of the Restoration and Rebuilding the Nation

The Dominican Republic now stood at a crossroads. It faced the formidable challenge of reviving an economy and landscape left battered by years of conflict. It was a time of rebuilding, of rolling up its sleeves and setting its sights on a future where prosperity was a shared dream.

Yet, this was no easy task. Resources were stretched thin, and the shadow of past conflicts lingered. The nation looked beyond its shores, seeking foreign investment to fuel its ambitions. Each step forward was measured, a delicate balance between aspiration and reality.

But the challenge was not just economic. The restoration of independence also cast a light on the deep social and regional divides that had long marked Dominican life. Efforts to bridge these gaps became a crucial part of the nation's journey, seeking to ensure that progress and opportunity reached every corner of the Republic. This era was about laying the groundwork for a society where every Dominican could find their place, disparities were acknowledged and addressed, and the promise of independence could be realized by all. Efforts were made to integrate various regions and communities into the national fabric, promoting a sense of unity and shared national identity.

Solidifying the Foundations of the Modern Dominican State

As the twentieth century unfolded, the Dominican Republic began reinforcing the pillars of a modern state. This was a time of both trials and triumphs, a period marked by the nation's collective effort to build a resilient and stable future.

There was a tangible push to weave a stronger political structure. Lawmakers, leaders, and judges worked together to fortify the nation's legislative, executive, and judicial branches. The evolution of political institutions wasn't just a matter of policy—it was about nurturing a democracy that truly reflected the Dominican people's diverse voices. The birth of new political parties and the move toward more inclusive elections were steps toward a future where every vote and every voice mattered.

The economic landscape was also shifting. The nation's leaders and entrepreneurs cast their eyes beyond the verdant fields of agriculture, aiming to diversify the economy. New industries began to emerge, drawing the interest of foreign investors and linking the Dominican Republic's fortunes to global markets. This economic growth, however, was a balancing act. The nation navigated the challenges of external dependencies and the ebbs and flows of the international economy.

In villages and cities alike, the government turned its attention to the well-being of its people. Efforts to bolster public health, education, and social welfare were more than policy initiatives; they were about lifting communities, bridging social divides, and building a society where every Dominican had the chance to thrive. The road to social equality and improved quality of life was often bumpy, with progress and setbacks walking hand in hand.

Amidst these changes, the Dominican Republic experienced a cultural renaissance. The arts flourished, literature blossomed, and music echoed the nation's soul. This cultural vibrancy was not just about entertainment; it was a celebration of the Dominican identity, a tapestry of history, values, and dreams woven into the everyday life of the people.

This era in the Dominican Republic's history was a defining one, a chapter where the nation solidified its foundations and strode confidently toward a future as a proud, diverse, and resilient state.

Navigating International Waters

On the international front, the Dominican Republic faced the challenge of maintaining sovereignty while engaging with more powerful nations, especially the United States. Navigating these relationships required diplomatic finesse and a firm commitment to national interests. The period saw various treaties and agreements, each reflecting the complex interplay between national sovereignty and international relations.

Despite the strides made, the Dominican Republic faced numerous challenges, including political instability, economic vulnerabilities, and social issues. However, the nation's progress in building a more stable and prosperous state was evident. The efforts and achievements of this period were instrumental in setting the Dominican Republic on its modern trajectory.

Reflecting on the Journey

The journey of the Dominican Republic in the late nineteenth and early twentieth centuries was one of transformation and resilience. From the turmoil of the Restoration War to the challenges of nation-building, the Dominican Republic's path to a modern state was marked by both trials and triumphs. This period laid the essential foundations for the nation's future development, reflecting the enduring spirit and determination of the Dominican people to build a stable, prosperous, and sovereign nation.

Chapter 8 – The American Intervention and Trujillo's Dictatorship

Now we enter the period in the Dominican Republic's history that's rife with American intervention and the notorious dictatorship of Rafael Trujillo. Spanning several decades of the twentieth century, this period encapsulates a crucial transformation in the nation's political, social, and cultural landscape. It's a period in history that strongly reflects the challenges of authoritarian rule, especially for a nation that still struggles to establish its identity and self-governance.

The American occupation, born out of geopolitical interests and internal turmoil, set in motion a series of changes that would deeply impact the Dominican Republic. It was an era where external forces and domestic aspirations intersected, shaping the nation's course in profound ways. Following this, the ascension and reign of Trujillo brought about a different set of dynamics. His rule, characterized by its iron grip and pervasive influence, left an indelible mark on the Dominican psyche and society.

These chapters in Dominican history are not just stories of control and governance; they are narratives of resilience, resistance, and the relentless pursuit of a democratic future. The shadow of Trujillo's regime, with its complexities and contradictions, and the nation's journey through and beyond it, paints a picture of a country grappling with its past while reaching for its future. The legacy of this era, with its blend of hardship and transformation, continues to echo in the Dominican Republic's ongoing narrative as a nation.

The Prelude to and Reasons for the United States Occupation

The early twentieth century in the Dominican Republic was a period that set the stage for one of the most significant foreign interventions in its history: the United States occupation of 1916-1924. Understanding the reasons for this occupation requires a look at both internal Dominican dynamics and broader geopolitical contexts of the era.

Internal Political and Economic Instability

In the Dominican Republic, the early twentieth century was a time of recurring political turbulence. The nation's landscape was dotted with local leaders and factions, each vying for control. This ongoing power struggle often led to periods of unrest and instability, posing challenges to the country's governance.

Economically, the situation was equally complex. The Dominican Republic grappled with the weight of substantial foreign debt and struggled to find steady ground for its fiscal policies. These economic hurdles left the country exposed to outside influence, affecting its financial independence and stability.

Dominican Government's Appeal for Assistance

Amid the Dominican Republic's internal conflicts and economic struggles, a faction, including some government officials, saw a potential lifeline in US intervention. They looked to America, hoping its involvement might stabilize the turbulent political scene, kickstart economic growth, and tackle the overwhelming burden of debt.

The United States, eyeing the situation, decided to step in. This move was driven by multiple motivations. With the introduction of policies like the Monroe Doctrine and the Roosevelt Corollary, the US demonstrated a keen interest in maintaining stability and safeguarding its interests in the Western Hemisphere. The opening of the Panama Canal and the outbreak of World War I only heightened this focus, placing the Caribbean, including the Dominican Republic, in a strategic position.

For the United States, a key concern was preventing European powers, especially Germany, from gaining influence in the Caribbean. The Dominican Republic's financial vulnerabilities could potentially offer a foothold for these powers. Amidst the global tensions of World

War I, the US was particularly vigilant, seeking to ensure that its sphere of influence in its backyard remained unchallenged by European nations.

This approach by the United States was part of a larger strategy known as "dollar diplomacy." The idea was to wield economic power and, when needed, direct intervention, to expand US influence.

The decision to intervene marked a turning point in Dominican history. It was a moment when the country's internal challenges collided with external interests, leading to significant repercussions.

The Unfolding and Immediate Outcomes of the United States Occupation

In 1916, the Dominican Republic experienced a pivotal moment in its history with the US occupation. This move brought profound changes to the nation. The United States stepped onto Dominican soil in an act driven by its own economic and strategic agenda rather than only the desire to help the struggling nation.

As American troops quickly reached Dominican soil and established a military government. They aimed to bring order and stability to a nation in turmoil. However, this new governance was met with a range of reactions among Dominicans. For some, it was a welcome intervention that promised stability. For others, it was a stark infringement on their sovereignty and a painful reminder of their loss of independence. However, any resistance was easily subdued by the US forces.

One of the central focuses of the US occupation was reshaping the Dominican economy. American authorities set their sights on stabilizing the nation's finances, restructuring its debt, and modernizing its financial systems. New fiscal policies were introduced, and American control over customs revenues began, aiming to use these funds to address foreign debts.

Beyond the economy, the occupation also ushered in a wave of infrastructure development. Roads were constructed, ports were enhanced, and sanitation facilities were improved. While these projects brought modernization to the Dominican Republic, they were often aligned more closely with American interests in the region than with the specific needs of the Dominican people.

The U.S. occupation was intended as a stabilizing force. While it succeeded on some level, it also brought a mix of advancement and challenges. It left a lasting impact on the Dominican Republic, affecting everything from governance and economics to the very landscape of the nation.

Impact on Dominican Society and Culture

The presence of American forces and administrators had a profound impact on Dominican society and culture. The occupation led to changes in social dynamics, with American cultural influences permeating various aspects of Dominican life.

It also sparked a sense of nationalism among many Dominicans, who resented the foreign control and perceived loss of their national identity. Resistance to the occupation manifested in various forms, from passive non-cooperation to active guerrilla warfare. Nationalist leaders and groups began to emerge, advocating for Dominican sovereignty and self-determination. This resistance played a crucial role in shaping the Dominican national consciousness and the eventual push for the end of the occupation.

Transition to Dominican Governance and Lasting Impact of the US Occupation

Moving from American control to Dominican rule was a key time in the Dominican Republic's history. The process was full of challenges, but it was vital for the country's future.

Resistance to the US occupation in the Dominican Republic grew over time. This, along with shifts in US foreign policy and the high costs of the occupation, led the Americans to rethink their military presence. Talks about pulling out US forces and handing control back to the Dominicans began. These talks focused on how to set up the new Dominican government, the military's role, and economic plans. Even as the US pulled out its troops, it aimed to keep some influence, especially in financial and diplomatic areas.

To move the Dominican Republic toward self-rule, a temporary government was set up. This government's job was to plan elections and manage the changeover. However, the impact of the US occupation and different ideas about what the Dominican Republic should become led to a lot of political back-and-forth during this time.

Elections and the Path to Democracy

The first elections after the occupation were a critical moment in the Dominican Republic's journey toward democracy. While these elections marked a significant step forward, the political landscape remained volatile, with factions and leaders from the occupation era continuing to wield considerable influence.

Economically, the post-occupation period required significant adjustments. The Dominican Republic had to manage its finances independently, address issues related to foreign debt, and rebuild an economy that had been heavily influenced by American policies and interests. Efforts were made to diversify the economy and promote sustainable growth.

Legacy of the US Occupation

Societally, the end of the occupation brought about a reassertion of Dominican culture and identity. The period of American control had introduced new cultural elements, but the return to self-governance saw a renewed emphasis on national traditions, customs, and values. This cultural renaissance played a key role in fostering a sense of national unity and pride.

The legacy of the US occupation in the Dominican Republic is complex. While it brought certain modernizations and reforms, it also left a lasting impact on the nation's political psyche. The experience of foreign control and the struggle for self-governance intensified nationalist sentiments and shaped the country's approach to international relations.

Rafael Trujillo's Rise to Power

Rafael Trujillo's rise to power marked a turning point in the Dominican Republic's history. His rise in the twentieth century started one of the nation's most notable and debated eras. Trujillo used political tactics, alliances, and strong control to climb to the top.

Trujillo started in the military, which had grown stronger during the American occupation. He moved up quickly, showing he was skilled and ambitious. His military experience and contacts were key in his push for political power.

In the late 1920s and early 1930s, Dominican politics were unstable. Governments changed often, and power struggles were common. Trujillo was smart in how he handled this situation. He used his military role to build alliances with important political figures and groups.

His control of the armed forces was essential in his rise. As head of the National Police, which later became the National Army, he gained a lot of power over the country's security and politics. This gave him tremendous influence and the ability to easily deal with any rivals.

The 1930 Presidential Election

In a pivotal moment in his rise to power, Rafael Trujillo easily took the 1930 election. His path to victory wasn't through fair means. Through a mix of shrewd political moves like silencing his opponents and widespread vote-rigging, his rise to power mimicked his rule. This election wasn't about the people's choice; it was a clear display of Trujillo's grip on the nation's political workings.

Trujillo wasted no time in setting up a dictatorial government. He quickly took control of every aspect of the state, leaving little room for opposition or dissent. His rule was marked by heavy-handed tactics. He imposed strict censorship and built a personality cult around himself. The government machinery was used not just to govern but to keep a tight hold on power.

Centralization of Power and Repression

Under this authoritarian rule, the Dominican Republic saw the rise of an authoritarian government with power concentrated at the top. Trujillo held sway over every government branch, ensuring that loyalty to him was the top priority in both the military and civil service. His regime became infamous for suppressing any political opposition. The Military Intelligence Service (SIM), functioning as Trujillo's secret police, was central to this crackdown. It conducted surveillance, intimidation, and even violence against those Trujillo saw as threats.

Economic development was a major focus of Trujillo's regime. He set out to modernize the economy, boost agricultural output, and foster industrial growth. Significant investments were made in building infrastructure like roads and public buildings. Yet, these economic efforts often had a dual purpose. They were as much about strengthening Trujillo's hold on power and enriching himself and his close associates as they were about national progress. Trujillo's personal control over large sectors of the economy was a testament to this.

Cultural and International Relations

Culturally, Trujillo sought to shape Dominican identity in a way that supported his regime. He promoted certain cultural expressions while suppressing others, particularly those he viewed as threatening to his vision of the nation. Internationally, Trujillo pursued relations that would bolster his regime's legitimacy and facilitate economic goals. He was adept at navigating the geopolitical landscape of the era, maintaining relations with the United States and other nations, even amidst growing concerns about his authoritarian rule.

Human Rights Abuses

The Trujillo regime was also marked by significant human rights abuses. These included the Parsley Massacre of 1937, in which thousands of Haitians living in the Dominican Republic were killed. Such acts of violence and repression were part of Trujillo's strategy to maintain control and instill fear in the population.

Weakening of Trujillo's Grip and Emerging Challenges

As Rafael Trujillo's long tenure progressed into the late 1950s, several factors began to converge, signaling a weakening of his once unassailable grip on the Dominican Republic. This segment explores the internal and external challenges that contributed to the erosion of Trujillo's power, setting the stage for significant changes in the country.

Within the Dominican Republic, the seeds of discontent were slowly germinating against Trujillo's oppressive regime. The harshness of his dictatorship began to alienate key segments of society. This shift in public sentiment was partly fueled by the brutality of actions such as the murder of the Mirabal sisters, which had a profound impact on the national consciousness.

Economic Decline and Mismanagement

Economically, the country faced challenges due to Trujillo's policies and mismanagement. While the regime had initially promoted economic growth, by the late 1950s, the benefits of this growth were unevenly distributed, with much of the wealth concentrated in Trujillo's hands and those of his close associates. Economic disparities and corruption led to dissatisfaction among the broader populace.

Trujillo's regime faced increasing isolation on the international stage. His involvement in plots against leaders of other countries, particularly in Venezuela, and the Dominican Republic's poor human rights record led to strained relations with neighboring nations and the United States. The shift in US foreign policy toward support for democracy and human rights under the Kennedy administration further isolated Trujillo.

Shifts in the Military and Elite

Crucially, there was a growing divide within the military and among the Dominican intellectuals and middle class. Some military leaders, who had been instrumental in maintaining Trujillo's rule, began to distance themselves from the dictator. This loss of support within the military, a cornerstone of Trujillo's power base, significantly weakened his position.

Opposition movements, both within the Dominican Republic and among exiled communities, gained momentum during this period. Underground resistance groups began to form more cohesive plans for challenging Trujillo's rule, seeking ways to bring about political change.

As these various challenges mounted, it became increasingly clear that Trujillo's regime was no longer as stable or invulnerable as it once had been. The combination of internal discontent, economic struggles, weakening support among the military and elites, and growing international isolation set the stage for a critical juncture in Dominican history.

The Assassination

The plot to assassinate Trujillo was orchestrated by a group of Dominicans, some of whom were close to the dictator but had grown disillusioned with his tyrannical rule. The plan involved careful coordination, as Trujillo's extensive intelligence network and control over the country made such an action risky and complex. The conspirators were motivated by a range of factors, from personal grievances to a desire to see democratic governance restored in the Dominican Republic.

On May 30, 1961, the plot came to fruition. Trujillo, traveling in his car on a road outside the capital city of Santo Domingo, was ambushed and killed. The assassination was a shock to the nation, abruptly ending the era of one of Latin America's most enduring dictators.

Immediate Response and Power Vacuum

Trujillo's assassination created an immediate power vacuum in the Dominican Republic. Trujillo's son, Ramfis Trujillo, initially attempted to take control, seeking to continue his father's legacy and maintain the family's grip on power. However, the regime's foundations were deeply shaken, and the assassination had unleashed forces that would prove difficult to contain.

Reactions

The news of Rafael Trujillo's assassination sent shockwaves through the Dominican Republic. The public reaction was divided. Some people grieved, losing the only leader they had known for many years. Others felt a sense of hope. They saw his death as a chance to end the oppression they had lived under.

The world also reacted to Trujillo's assassination. The United States saw it as a chance for democracy in the Dominican Republic. But there was worry, too. They feared what the change might mean for stability in the Caribbean.

Navigating Post-Trujillo Turbulence and the Path to Democracy

In the aftermath of Rafael Trujillo's assassination, the Dominican Republic faced a period of significant turbulence as it navigated the challenging transition from dictatorship to democracy.

Different groups started competing for control. Trujillo's former supporters, military factions, and new groups wanting democracy all jumped into the fray. The country experienced several leadership changes, with many short-term governments and power struggles.

This unrest caught the attention of the United States. In 1965, it sent military forces to the Dominican Republic. The US was worried about Communism spreading, especially during the Cold War. Their intervention was a major event that led to a civil war. Forces who supported Juan Bosch, the president who was removed from power, fought against a government backed by the military.

Restoration of Civilian Rule

The civil war in the Dominican Republic and the involvement of the US led to a significant shift. Eventually, both sides reached a compromise, paving the way for civilian leadership.

In the years after Trujillo, the Dominican Republic experienced major economic shifts and focused on social progress. There were efforts to diversify the economy beyond traditional sectors, to build better infrastructure, and to tackle social challenges. However, these changes happened against a backdrop of ongoing political ups and downs. The country's internal politics were often influenced by global events and trends.

The post-Trujillo era also witnessed cultural shifts as the Dominican Republic sought to redefine its national identity in the absence of the pervasive cult of personality. There was a renewed focus on cultural expression, historical reevaluation, and the celebration of Dominican heritage, free from the shadow of dictatorship.

Gradual Move Toward Democracy

After Trujillo's regime ended, the Dominican Republic slowly moved toward democracy. This journey wasn't easy. The nation faced many difficulties, including times of harsh rule and political turmoil. Despite these hurdles, progress was made. The country worked to build democratic institutions, conduct elections, and nurture a society where people could actively participate in politics.

Chapter 9 – The Path Toward Modern Democracy

Formerly an ambassador and then vice president during Trujillo's dictatorship, Joaquin Balaguer not only served multiple terms as the Dominican Republic's first democratic ruler but also brought the country into a new era. Democracy hasn't come easy to the island, and the path is still unfinished, but this was the first step of many in the country's journey to finding itself.

Joaquin Balaguer's Rise to Power and Leadership Style

Joaquin Balaguer's rise to the presidency in 1966 was a key moment for the Dominican Republic after years of instability. Since Balaguer had worked with Rafael Trujillo before, people had different views about what he would do.

Balaguer's leadership style was mixed. He did a lot to modernize the country, and these changes helped the country grow. He also tried to make the economy stronger and more diverse, moving beyond just farming. But Balaguer's way of ruling had issues. He kept tight control over politics and did not always let people speak freely or oppose him. The media and political groups often found it hard to work under his rules. This made some people worry about how much freedom they really had.

Balaguer was president on and off for about thirty years. His way of mixing development with strict control made his time as a leader complex, and people still debate his presidency. He helped the country grow, but he also held back some changes that could have made the Dominican Republic more democratic.

Balaguer's Policies and Their Impact on Dominican Politics

Joaquin Balaguer's time as president was marked by specific policies that shaped the Dominican Republic. He focused on economic stability and growth. This meant building industries beyond agriculture. He also worked on big projects like roads and public buildings. But these projects weren't just about growth. They also helped Balaguer keep power.

Balaguer's rule happened during the Cold War when the United States and the Soviet Union were in a global struggle for influence. The US wanted to stop Communism from spreading and saw Balaguer as a key ally in the Caribbean. Balaguer used this to his advantage. He got support from the US, which helped him stay in power longer.

Domestically, Balaguer's policies had mixed effects. Some people saw him as a leader who brought development. Others criticized him for not doing enough for democracy.

Balaguer's style of leadership left a lasting mark on Dominican politics. After him, leaders had to balance growth with more democracy. They also had to think about how to deal with other countries, especially the United States. Balaguer showed that a leader could drive change but also that power needed limits.

Democratic Shifts and Changes in the Dominican Republic

Following Joaquin Balaguer's long tenure, the Dominican Republic entered a period of significant political transformation. In the late twentieth century, the nation gradually shifted toward a more democratic system. This transition was characterized by a series of reforms and political changes that marked a departure from the authoritarian past.

The first major sign of democratic change was the move toward fairer and more transparent elections. The electoral process, previously marred by fraud and manipulation, began to open. No longer just routine exercises, elections were transforming into true reflections of the people's will. This was democracy in action—making sure that every vote counted, and every voice was heard. These reforms aimed to build public trust in the electoral process, a crucial step in consolidating democracy. Voter education campaigns and improvements in election management helped ensure that elections truly reflected the will of the people.

These changes were crucial in allowing different political parties and candidates to participate more actively in the political process. The Dominican political landscape started to diversify during this period. New political parties emerged, representing a range of ideologies and interests. This shift broke the monopoly of power and allowed for a more pluralistic political dialogue. The rise of these new parties also meant that the Dominican people had more choices and could hold their leaders more accountable.

In its pursuit of a stronger democracy, the Dominican Republic placed great emphasis on fortifying the pillars of its society. Key among these were the judicial and legislative systems, vital cogs in the machinery of a fair and democratic state.

The focus on the judiciary was about more than legal structures. It was about nurturing a system where justice wasn't just a concept but a living, breathing reality. Efforts were channeled into ensuring that judges could make decisions independently, free from external pressures. Laws needed to be more than words on paper; they had to be fair and consistently applied, giving every citizen a sense of trust and equality before the law.

Legislation, too, saw a wave of change. Gone were the days when laws were shaped in closed rooms. The goal was to peel back the curtains, letting in transparency and a chorus of diverse voices. Law-making became a more inclusive process, inviting different perspectives and ensuring that laws reflected the rich tapestry of the nation's populace.

Addressing Social and Economic Challenges

An additional change with the democratic shift was the strengthening of civil society. The Dominican Republic worked to address the inequalities that had long been a part of its society. Initiatives in education, health, and social welfare sought to reduce disparities and ensure that all citizens had the opportunity to contribute to and benefit from the nation's growth.

Non-governmental organizations, community groups, and advocacy groups became more active and influential. These organizations played a critical role in holding the government accountable and advocating for various social issues. Additionally, the media began to enjoy greater freedom, becoming an essential tool for information and public discourse.

To support this new government agenda, the economy needed to change. The goal was clear: build an open, varied, and robust economy. The nation set its sights on drawing in foreign investors, nurturing local businesses, protecting local industries and workers' rights, and moving beyond its traditional reliance on agriculture. These economic reforms weren't just about numbers and policies; they were about lifting people's lives, making sure the fruits of democracy could be felt in everyday living, from better jobs to reduced poverty.

The Path of Resilience and Hope

Despite these efforts, the path to a fully realized democracy was marked by hurdles. Corruption remained an issue, requiring ongoing vigilance and reform. Political stability was occasionally threatened by internal and external pressures, reminding the nation of the fragility of its democratic gains. And then there were the lingering social inequalities, a stark reminder of the gaps that still needed bridging.

Yet, through these challenges, the Dominican Republic demonstrated resilience and hope. Leaders and citizens alike were actively shaping a political scene that was once dominated by singular, authoritarian rule. This was a time of redefining what the nation stood for and how it would govern itself in the years to come. Civil society organizations grew stronger, playing a key role in advocating for democratic principles and holding leaders accountable. Media freedom continued to be a vital part of the democratic landscape, providing a platform for public discourse and scrutiny.

As the century turned, the Dominican Republic stood as a nation increasingly confident in its democratic journey. The lessons learned from overcoming past challenges informed its path forward. The country's commitment to nurturing democratic principles, addressing socio-economic disparities, and fostering a vibrant civil society continued to shape its pursuit of a stable, inclusive, and prosperous future.

The Dynamic Impact of the Dominican Diaspora

As the Dominican Republic journeyed toward a democratic future, the voices and actions of its diaspora community became increasingly influential. Spread across the globe, especially in the United States, these expatriate Dominicans were not just passive observers but active participants in shaping their homeland's destiny.

Economically, the diaspora was a lifeline. The money they sent back home went beyond just supporting families. These remittances became a key economic driver, helping to stabilize and grow the Dominican economy.

Culturally, the diaspora kept the Dominican spirit alive across continents. They shared the rhythms of merengue and bachata, the flavors of Dominican cuisine, and the vibrancy of Caribbean art with the world. This cultural exchange not only showcased the Dominican heritage globally but also kept the diaspora connected to their roots.

Dominicans abroad found themselves in a unique position to impact the politics back home. They brought fresh perspectives, shaped by their experiences in diverse political environments. Through advocacy and dialogue, they pushed for democratic reforms and greater respect for human rights in the Dominican Republic. Their involvement added a new layer to the political discourse, bridging the local and global contexts. Their influence sometimes extended to shaping the foreign policy of these nations toward their homeland.

The ability to vote in national elections from abroad further empowered the diaspora. This right ensured that their voices were heard in the electoral process, adding a new dimension to the Dominican Republic's democratic journey.

Integrating the diaspora's perspective into the national dialogue wasn't always smooth. There were times when their views clashed with those living in the Dominican Republic, creating tensions over the direction of the country's future.

Despite these occasional frictions, the role of the Dominican diaspora in the late twentieth and early twenty-first centuries was undeniably pivotal. They were more than just a community living abroad; they were partners in the Dominican Republic's progress toward a more democratic, economically robust, and culturally rich nation. Their contributions were a clear reflection of the interconnected world we live in and the power of a global community to influence change both at home and abroad.

The Evolving Role of the Dominican Diaspora in Nation Building

In the early twenty-first century, the influence of the Dominican diaspora continued to evolve, playing a critical role in the nation-building process of the Dominican Republic. This vibrant community, though physically distant, remained deeply connected to their homeland, contributing to its development in multifaceted ways.

The political involvement of the diaspora became more nuanced over time. They not only participated in elections but also began to engage in more substantive policy discussions. Many in the diaspora sought to address issues like corruption and governance, which directly impacted their families and communities back home. Their external perspective provided a valuable counterpoint to the internal political discourse, offering solutions informed by a blend of local understanding and international experience.

Beyond sending remittances, Dominicans abroad started to invest more directly in the economy. They ventured into sectors like technology, renewable energy, and tourism, diversifying the economic landscape of the Dominican Republic. This entrepreneurial spirit helped create jobs and fostered a more dynamic economy. The diaspora's investment in local businesses also promoted a culture of entrepreneurship within the country, inspiring a new generation of Dominican entrepreneurs.

Cultural Exchange and Identity

The diaspora continued to play a vital role in cultural exchange, promoting Dominican culture on a global stage. They became instrumental in organizing cultural festivals, music events, and art exhibitions that not only celebrated Dominican heritage but also facilitated cultural dialogues with other communities. This exchange enriched the Dominican identity, making it more inclusive and diverse.

Education emerged as a key area where the diaspora made substantial contributions. Through scholarships, mentorship programs, and academic partnerships, they facilitated knowledge transfer and educational opportunities for Dominicans in the homeland. These initiatives helped bridge educational gaps and prepared the younger generation for global competitiveness.

The diaspora's advocacy efforts expanded to include broader social issues such as healthcare, women's rights, and environmental sustainability. By leveraging their positions in host countries, they brought attention and resources to these critical areas, aiding in the social development of the Dominican Republic.

Facing New Challenges

As the Dominican diaspora's role grew, so did the challenges. Ensuring that their contributions aligned with the country's needs required continuous dialogue and collaboration. Moreover, maintaining cultural connections across generations posed its own set of challenges, as younger members of the diaspora navigated their dual identities.

The Dominican diaspora's role in the early twenty-first century was marked by an expanding scope and deepening impact. They became not just participants but key players in shaping the Dominican Republic's journey toward a more prosperous, democratic, and culturally vibrant society. Their story is a testament to the profound impact that a global community can have on its homeland, shaping its future through a blend of love, commitment, and shared vision.

Chapter 10 – The Dominican Republic and the Modern Era

The Dominican Republic has undergone significant political changes recently. It's moving away from its past dominated by strong leaders. Now, it's on a path to a stronger, more vibrant democracy. Of course, the path to a stronger democracy isn't without its hurdles. Tackling these issues is key to maintaining the momentum of democratic progress.

Shifts in Political Dynamics

In the Dominican Republic's ongoing democratic evolution, recent years have seen a notable shift in political dynamics. This shift reflects a growing emphasis on addressing longstanding challenges while navigating new ones in an ever-changing global landscape.

Focus on Addressing Corruption

One of the critical challenges has been combating corruption, which has long plagued Dominican politics. Recent administrations have taken steps to tackle this issue, implementing measures to increase transparency and hold public officials accountable. Anti-corruption initiatives have gained momentum, with a focus on strengthening legal frameworks and enhancing the independence of oversight institutions.

Political Stability and Governance

The country has also worked on improving political stability. Efforts to strengthen democratic governance are visible. Political institutions are being fortified to work effectively and independently. The aim is to create a political environment where policies and decisions are made for the public good, not personal gain. Making the government more open and responsible has been central to this change. The country is reforming how elections work. The goal is to make elections fair and truly reflect the people's choices. These changes are building trust in the political system. They also help make the transfer of power smoother.

There's more diversity in politics now than ever before. Many new parties and groups are emerging, bringing a variety of ideas and viewpoints. This is enriching political discussions and making them more inclusive. Civil society groups are becoming stronger. They act as watchdogs and push for better policies. They keep the government in check and make sure it listens to its people.

Youth and Political Engagement

Another significant development is the increasing political involvement of the Dominican youth. Young people are more engaged than ever, bringing new energy and perspectives to political discourse. They are actively participating in political processes, advocating for issues like education, employment, and climate change.

International Relations and Diplomacy

The Dominican Republic's evolving relationship with the world has also influenced its political development. Strong ties with global powers, especially the United States, and active participation in international organizations have shaped policies at home. These relationships have brought both opportunities and challenges.

The Dominican Republic continues to navigate its diplomatic relationships carefully. The country is balancing its traditional alliances while seeking new partnerships. These international relations are crucial in a globalized world where foreign policy impacts domestic issues like trade, security, and immigration.

Preparing for Future Challenges

As it prepares for future challenges, the Dominican Republic is focusing on building a resilient political system. This involves adapting to global economic shifts, technological advancements, and environmental concerns. The goal is to ensure that the nation's political framework is robust enough to handle future uncertainties.

As we've seen, the Dominican Republic's recent political journey is marked by efforts to strengthen democratic practices, combat corruption, and engage its youth. As the country continues to grow on the international stage, its commitment to improving governance and stability remains a priority. These efforts are crucial in shaping a future where the Dominican Republic can thrive as a stable, democratic, and prosperous nation in the global community.

Looking to the future, the Dominican Republic stands at an exciting crossroads. It's a time of opportunity to solidify democratic gains, tackle existing challenges, and embrace the potential of a more engaged and empowered society. The nation's political story is still being written, each chapter reflecting a commitment to deepening democracy and responding to the evolving aspirations of its people.

The Dominican Republic Today

In the Dominican Republic's recent history, remarkable strides in economic growth and social development stand out. The country has moved beyond its traditional agricultural base, branching into diverse sectors like manufacturing and services. Special economic zones have attracted foreign investments, boosting exports and broadening the economic landscape.

Tourism has blossomed, becoming a cornerstone of the economy. The Dominican Republic's natural beauty and rich culture now draw visitors from around the world. This boom in tourism has not only increased revenue but also created countless jobs, contributing significantly to the nation's prosperity.

The realm of international trade has also seen dynamic changes. The Dominican Republic's involvement in free trade agreements has opened doors to new markets, enhancing its role in regional trade. Yet, with economic success come challenges like income inequality and uneven regional development. These issues are at the forefront, demanding solutions that ensure growth benefits all.

In social spheres, progress is visible but accompanied by enduring challenges. Education and healthcare have seen improvements through increased investments and reforms. However, issues like educational quality and healthcare access remain, calling for continued dedication and innovation.

Culturally, the Dominican Republic is experiencing a renaissance. Its music, literature, and arts are not just thriving domestically but also capturing the world's imagination, showcasing the vibrant Dominican spirit.

Environmental sustainability and climate change have become pressing concerns. The country is actively seeking ways to address these global challenges, recognizing their impact on the future.

Technology's growing influence is unmistakable. It's opening new avenues in education, business, and governance, signaling a shift toward a more connected and digital future.

As the Dominican Republic progresses, it's a balancing act between celebrating achievements and tackling ongoing challenges. The nation's journey is one of evolution, marked by a commitment to building a prosperous, equitable, and sustainable future for all its citizens.

Conclusion

As we look back on the Dominican Republic's rich and multifaceted history, it becomes clear that the nation's journey has been one of adaptation and continuous transformation. From its roots in the indigenous Taíno culture to its complex colonial past, the trials of dictatorship, and the triumphs of democratic progress, the Dominican Republic's story is a tapestry of struggle and success, setbacks and breakthroughs.

The history of the Dominican Republic is a narrative marked by resilience. The struggles against colonial powers, the battles for independence, and the enduring fight against dictatorship have all shaped the nation's character. This resilience is not just seen in the grand moments of revolution or change but in the everyday lives of the Dominican people who have navigated these turbulent waters with unwavering spirit and hope.

The transformation from a country once weighed down by authoritarian rule to one that embraces democratic ideals is a significant achievement. The Dominican Republic's path toward democracy has been neither straightforward nor easy. It has involved a complex interplay of internal aspirations and external influences, each step reflective of a nation striving to realize its potential.

Economically, the Dominican Republic has evolved from a primarily agricultural society to one that embraces modernity and diversity. Its growth in tourism, industry, and international trade marks a shift toward a more interconnected and dynamic economic model. Yet, the journey here, too, has been one of balancing growth with equity, ensuring that the resulting prosperity reaches all corners of society.

Socially, the country has seen significant strides in education, healthcare, and civil rights. These advancements are fundamental to the nation's progress, yet the journey continues as the Dominican Republic seeks to bridge the gaps that still exist within its society.

Culturally, the Dominican Republic stands as a beacon of diversity and vibrancy. The fusion of Taíno, African, and Spanish influences has given rise to a unique cultural identity—one that is celebrated not just within the nation but also by the global Dominican diaspora. This cultural richness is a testament to the country's ability to blend traditions and influences into a distinct and captivating tapestry.

Reflecting on the Dominican Republic's historical journey, it's evident that the nation has not only weathered many storms but has also harnessed these experiences to forge a path of growth and renewal. The lessons learned, the challenges overcome, and the successes achieved all paint a picture of a nation that is continually evolving, resiliently facing its past while confidently looking toward the future.

The Dominican Republic today is more than just a country with a rich past. It's actively shaping who it is in the Caribbean and the wider world. This nation mixes its history with the present. It brings together tradition and innovation. It connects local life with global trends. This makes the Dominican Republic unique in today's interconnected world.

In the Caribbean, the Dominican Republic is a beacon of growth and resilience. It faces the same challenges as its neighbors, like changing economies and climate risks, yet it adds to the region's cultural and social life. The country works with others in the area to grow and find stability. It shows a commitment to not just itself but to the well-being of the entire Caribbean.

Globally, the Dominican Republic is earning recognition. Its role in trade is growing, thanks to its location. The country is a key player in the world's markets. It's also active in global discussions, talking about climate change, trade, and development. This shows its influence and willingness to be part of solving global issues.

As the world changes, the Dominican Republic keeps its traditions alive while embracing new ideas. This balance is key to its identity. The country offers a unique view to the world. It values its history and is open to new possibilities.

Dominicans living abroad help shape how the world sees their country. They spread Dominican culture and build understanding globally. Their efforts, from sending money home to cultural sharing and political involvement, are a big part of the Dominican Republic's story on the world stage.

Looking ahead, the Dominican Republic is ready for innovation, sustainability, and including everyone in its growth. It's set to face new challenges while capturing opportunities. The Dominican Republic's journey is a story of constant change. It's a country that knows where it comes from and is excited about where it's going.

If you enjoyed this book, a review on Amazon would be greatly appreciated because it would mean a lot to hear from you.

To leave a review:

1. Open your camera app.
2. Point your mobile device at the QR code.
3. The review page will appear in your web browser.

Thanks for your support!

Here's another book by Captivating History that you might like

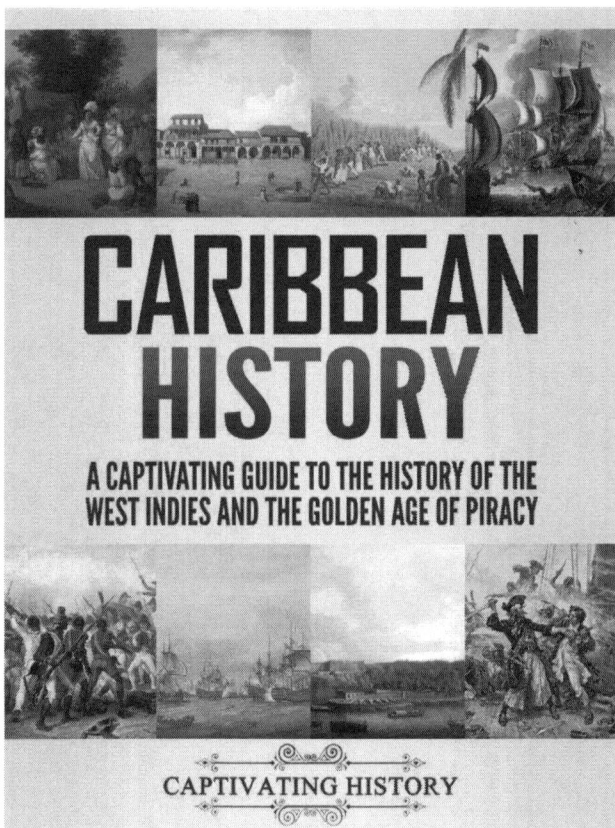

CARIBBEAN HISTORY

A CAPTIVATING GUIDE TO THE HISTORY OF THE WEST INDIES AND THE GOLDEN AGE OF PIRACY

CAPTIVATING HISTORY

Free Bonus from Captivating History
(Available for a Limited time)

Hi History Lovers!

Now you have a chance to join our exclusive history list so you can get your first history ebook for free as well as discounts and a potential to get more history books for free!

Simply visit the link below to join.

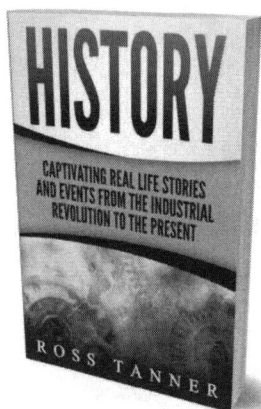

Or, Scan the QR code!

captivatinghistory.com/ebook

Also, make sure to follow us on Facebook, X, and YouTube by searching for Captivating History.

References

Chapter 1

"Hispaniola" https://www.newworldencyclopedia.org/entry/Hispaniola Accessed: November 6, 2023.

"Who Were the Taíno, the Original Inhabitants of Columbus' Island Colonies?" https://www.smithsonianmag.com/history/who-were-taino-original-inhabitants-columbus-island-73824867/ Accessed: November 6, 2023.

"Peopling of the Americas" https://www.pnas.org/post/podcast/peopling-americas Accessed: November 6, 2023.

"The Indigenous Peoples" https://www.globalsecurity.org/military/world/cuba/indigenous.htm Accessed: November 6, 2023.

Baver, Sherrie and Lisa Paravisini-Gebert. "Hispaniola's Environmental Story: Challenging and Iconic Image." *Callaloo* 37, no. 3 (2014): 648-661.

Chapter 2

"Who Were the Taíno, the Original Inhabitants of Columbus' Island Colonies?" https://www.smithsonianmag.com/history/who-were-taino-original-inhabitants-columbus-island-73824867/ Accessed: November 6, 2023.

"Taíno Culture History" https://www.floridamuseum.ufl.edu/histarch/research/haiti/en-bas-saline/taino-culture/ Accessed: November 8, 2023.

"Taíno Society" https://www.floridamuseum.ufl.edu/histarch/research/haiti/en-bas-saline/taino-society/ Accessed: November 8, 2023.

"History" https://tainomuseum.org/taino/history/ Accessed: November 8, 2023.

"Taino words in the Spanish Language" https://iic-spanish.com/en/taino-words-in-the-spanish-language/ Accessed: November 8, 2023.

"Study puts the 'Carib' in 'Caribbean,' boosting credibility of Columbus' cannibal claims" https://www.floridamuseum.ufl.edu/science/carib-skulls-boost-credibility-of-columbus-cannibal-claims/ Accessed: November 8, 2023.

"Who are the Carib People?" https://massacre.omeka.net/exhibits/show/the-kalinago--carib--people/the-kalinagos Accessed: November 8, 2023.

"Meet the Kalinago" https://discoverdominica.com/en/places/67/kalinago-territory Accessed: November 8, 2023.

Chapter 3

"Columbus 525: An Exploration of Christopher Columbus's Impact on the Atlantic World" https://www.haiti.org/columbus-525-an-exploration-of-christopher-columbuss-impact-on-the-atlantic-world/ Accessed: November 10, 2023.

"The First in the Indies" https://nationalhumanitiescenter.org/pds/amerbegin/settlement/text1/Columbus Hispaniola.pdf Accessed: November 10, 2023.

"Oct 12, 1492 CE: Columbus Makes Landfall in the Caribbean" https://education.nationalgeographic.org/resource/columbus-makes-landfall-caribbean/ Accessed: November 10, 2023.

"The Second Voyage of Christopher Columbus" https://www.thoughtco.com/the-second-voyage-of-christopher-columbus-2136700 Accessed: November 10, 2023.

"La Isabela" https://www.floridamuseum.ufl.edu/histarch/research/dominican-republic/la-isabela/ Accessed: November 10, 2023.

"Concepcion de la Vega: Columbus's Forgotten City" https://www.floridamuseum.ufl.edu/histarch/research/dominican-republic/concepcion-de-la-vega/ Accessed: November 10, 2023.

"Spain's American Colonies and the Encomienda System" https://www.thoughtco.com/spains-american-colonies-encomienda-system-2136545 Accessed: November 10, 2023.

"Enriquillo" http://hiaw.org/defcon2/lam/inddom15191533.html Accessed: November 10, 2023.

Chapter 4

Ponce Vazquez, J. "Colonial Origins: Hispaniola in the Sixteenth Century. In *Islanders and Empire: Smuggling and Political Defiance in Hispaniola, 1580-1690*, 22-55. Cambridge; Cambridge University Press, 2020.

"Sugar & the Rise of the Plantation System"
https://www.worldhistory.org/article/1784/sugar--the-rise-of-the-plantation-system/ Accessed: November 12, 2023.

"Santo Domingo: The city that kept slavery silent"
https://www.bbc.com/travel/article/20201117-santo-domingo-the-city-that-kept-slavery-silent Accessed: November 12, 2023.

"La Espanola: the earliest recorded Blacks in the Colonial Americas"
https://about.jstor.org/blog/la-espanola-the-earliest-recorded-blacks-in-the-early-colonial-americas/ Accessed: November 12, 2023.

"The 1521 Santo Domingo Slave Revolt" https://www.blackpast.org/global-african-history/the-1521-santo-domingo-slave-revolt/ Accessed: November 12, 2023.

"Caribbean Racial Formations"
https://eaop.ucsd.edu/198/pigmentocracy/Caribbean%20Racial%20Formations%20-%20CARIBBEAN%20SOCIAL%20STRUCTURE,%20CARIBBEAN%20POLITICAL%20CULTURE,%20MIDDLE-CLASS%20HEGEMONY%20-%20System,%20Black,%20Classes,%20and%20Plantation%20-%20JRank%20Articles.pdf Accessed: November 12, 2023.

Chapter 5

"Who were the real pirates of the Caribbean?"
https://www.rmg.co.uk/stories/topics/who-were-real-pirates-caribbean Accessed: November 14, 2023.

"The Golden Age of Piracy" https://www.rmg.co.uk/stories/topics/golden-age-piracy Accessed: November 14, 2023.

"Tortuga: The Pirate Stronghold"
https://www.heritagedaily.com/2020/12/tortuga-the-pirate-stronghold/136613 Accessed: November 14, 2023.

"The Buccaneers" http://www.cindyvallar.com/buccaneers.html Accessed: November 14, 2023.

"Sir Henry Morgan" https://www.historic-uk.com/HistoryUK/HistoryofWales/Sir-Henry-Morgan/ Accessed: November 14, 2023.

"Blackbeard: History of the Dreaded Pirate"
https://www.qaronline.org/history/blackbeard-history-dreaded-pirate Accessed: November 14, 2023.

"Jean Lafitte: History & Mystery"
https://www.nps.gov/jela/learn/historyculture/jean-lafitte-history-mystery.htm Accessed: November 14, 2023.

"The Women Pirates of the Caribbean: Anne Bonny and Mary Read" https://sillyhistory.com/2015/01/24/the-women-pirates-of-the-caribbean-anne-bonny-and-mary-read/ Accessed: November 14, 2023.

Hinckley, Theodore C. "The Decline of Caribbean Smuggling." *Journal of Inter-American Studies* 5, no. 1 (1963): 107-121.

"Spain's Rivals Emerge" https://courses.lumenlearning.com/suny-ushistory1ay/chapter/spains-rivals-emerge/ Accessed: November 14, 2023.

Chapter 6

"Haitian Revolution (1791-1804)" https://www.blackpast.org/global-african-history/haitian-revolution-1791-1804/ Accessed: November 17, 2023

"How Toussaint L'ouverture Rose from Slavery to Lead the Haitian Revolution" https://www.history.com/news/toussaint-louverture-haiti-revolution Accessed: November 17, 2023.

"Jean-Jacques Dessalines (1758-1806)" https://www.blackpast.org/global-african-history/dessalines-jean-jacques-1758-1806/ Accessed: November 17, 2023.

"Henri Christophe (1767-1820)" https://www.blackpast.org/global-african-history/henri-christophe-1767-1820/#:~:text=Henri%20Christophe%20was%20a%20military,Domingue%2C%20most%20likely%20from%20Kitts Accessed: November 17, 2023.

"Haitian and Dominican Freedom Struggles in the Nineteenth Century" https://www.aaihs.org/haitian-and-dominican-freedom-struggles-in-the-nineteenth-century/ Accessed: November 17, 2023.

"Santo Domingo's Struggle for Independence from Haiti" https://www.historytoday.com/archive/santo-domingos-struggle-independence-haiti Accessed: November 17, 2023.

"Here's the Truth About Dominican Independence Day" https://www.refinery29.com/en-us/2021/02/10334054/dominican-republic-independence-day-history-haiti Accessed: November 17, 2023.

"La Trinitaria, The Secret Society That Led to the Independence of the Dominican Republic" https://nuestrostories.com/2022/11/la-trinitaria-secret-society-dominican-republic/ Accessed: November 17, 2023.

"Juan Pablo Duarte" http://www.famousamericans.net/juanpabloduarte/ Accessed: November 17, 2023.

"Mella: a leading patriot in independence and restoration" https://dominicantoday.com/dr/local/2023/02/25/mella-a-leading-patriot-in-independence-and-restoration/ Accessed: November 17, 2023.

"Francisco del Rosario Sánchez (1817-1861)" https://www.blackpast.org/global-african-history/francisco-del-rosario-sanchez-1817-1861/ Accessed: November 17, 2023.

"Santana, Pedro (1801-1864)"
https://www.encyclopedia.com/humanities/encyclopedias-almanacs-transcripts-and-maps/santana-pedro-1801-1864 Accessed: November 17, 2023.

Chapter 7

"Annexation by Spain, 1861-65" https://countrystudies.us/dominican-republic/6.htm Accessed: November 20, 2023.

"Dominican Republic Restoration Day – August 16th"
https://www.vamosforschools.co.uk/hispanic-world/history/dominican-republic-restoration-day/ Accessed: November 20, 2023.

"Dominican Republic: Annexation by Spain, 1861-65" http://www.country-data.com/cgi-bin/query/r-3786.html Accessed: November 20, 2023.

"War of Restoration in the Dominican Republic 1861-1865"
https://onwar.com/data/dominican1861.html Accessed: November 20, 2023.

Chapter 8

"Rafael Trujillo" https://www.biography.com/political-figures/rafael-trujillo Accessed: November 22, 2023.

"Dominican activists challenge Rafael Trujillo's dictatorship (Fourteenth of June Movement), 1959-1960"
https://nvdatabase.swarthmore.edu/content/dominican-activists-challenge-rafael-trujillo-s-dictatorship-fourteenth-june-movement-1959-1 Accessed: November 22, 2023.

"Rafael Leonidas Trujillo"
https://www.nypl.org/sites/default/files/blog_attachments/TrujilloBio.pdf Accessed: November 22, 2023.

"Dominican Republic, 1916-1924" https://2001-2009.state.gov/r/pa/ho/time/wwi/108649.htm#:~:text=Triggered%20by%20concerns%20about%20possible,which%20would%20last%20until%201924 Accessed: November 22, 2023.

"US Occupation of the Dominican Republic" https://www.thoughtco.com/us-occupation-of-the-dominican-republic-2136380 Accessed: November 22, 2023.

"Remembering to Never Forget: Dominican Republic's 'Parsley Massacre'"
https://www.npr.org/sections/thetwo-way/2012/10/01/162092252/remembering-to-never-forget-dominican-republics-parsley-massacre Accessed: November 22, 2023.

Chapter 9

"Joaquin Balaguer" https://www.britannica.com/biography/Joaquin-Balaguer Accessed: November 25, 2023.

"Joaquin Balaguer"
https://www.oxfordreference.com/display/10.1093/oi/authority.2011080309544
2210 Accessed: November 25, 2023.

"Dominican Republic (1902-present)"
https://uca.edu/politicalscience/home/research-projects/dadm-project/western-
hemisphere-region/dominican-republic-1902-present/ Accessed: November 25,
2023.

Tillman, Ellen D. "The Dominican Republic: From Military Rule to
Democracy" *Oxford Research Encyclopedia of Politics*, February 23, 2021.
https://oxfordre.com/politics/view/10.1093/acrefore/9780190228637.001.0001/
acrefore-9780190228637-e-1811 Accessed: November 25, 2023.

"How Democracy is Succeeding" https://www.usglc.org/blog/how-democracy-is-
succeeding/ Accessed: November 25, 2023.

Mayes, April. *The Mulatto Republic: Class, Race, and Dominican National
Identity.* Gainesville: University Press of Florida, 2014.

"Not Everyone Who Speaks Spanish is from Spain: Taino Survival in the 21ˢᵗ
Century Dominican Republic"
https://web.archive.org/web/20040617195321/http://www.kacike.org/FerbelEng
lish.pdf Accessed: November 25, 2023.

"World Directory of Minorities and Indigenous Peoples – Dominican
Republic" https://www.refworld.org/cgi-
bin/texis/vtx/rwmain?page=country&category=&publisher=&type=COUNTRY
PROF&coi=DOM&rid=&docid=4954ce1923&skip=0 Accessed: November 25,
2023.

"Dominican Republic" https://www.iom.int/countries/dominican-republic
Accessed: November 25, 2023.

Chapter 10

"Exploring Dominican Culture" https://www.afsusa.org/countries/dominican-
republic/ Accessed: November 27, 2023.

"Dominican Republic: Bearing Witness to a Modern Genocide"
https://clacs.berkeley.edu/dominican-republic-bearing-witness-modern-genocide
Accessed: November 27, 2023.

"Dominican Republic" https://freedomhouse.org/country/dominican-
republic/freedom-world/2022 Accessed: November 27, 2023.

Made in the USA
Middletown, DE
05 December 2024